Shovel Supporters

GOD TIER SUPPORTERS

Alison Nilson
Andrew Brown
Angelo Sciarra
Ben Appleton
Geoffrey Jones
Jane Kift
John Connolly
Judith Daley
Margaret Lehmann
Michael Linehan
Tricia Eagleton

GOLD SUPPORTERS

Bob Fowler
Adrienne Williams
Alalasunderam Navaratnam
Alan J Vivian
Alan Millard
Alan Robertson
Alex Ghanem
Alexandra Foresto
Aline
Andrew Lawson
Andrew Putt
Andy Forgan
Ange Casey
Angela Burns
Angela Douglas
Ann Gee
Ann M Herriot
Anna Foale
Ashley Yelds
Barbara Gleeson
Ben Barnes
Beth Mohle
Beverly Houterman
Bill Malone
Bob Bunnett
Brad Bellette
Brendan McPhillips
Brett Drayton
Brett Inder
Brett Pereira
Brett Wiggins
Brigida Irving
Bronwen Machin
Brook Turner
Bruce Pollock
Carly Harvey
Carol Ladd
Caroline Buckingham
Catherine Beacham
Catherine Ganley
Catherine Jenkins
Cathie Williams
Charles Brown
Chris Bain
Chris Cook
Chris Ewart
Chris Nyland
Christopher Thomas
Clem Hedemann
Cosimo Borrelli
Courtney Roche
Craig Butters
Craig Lenehan
Craig Stokoe
Damian Lydon
Daniel Baxter
David Ball
David Brindley
David Griffin
David Hay
David Marr
Dawn Rowan
Dawn Rowan
Dean Pavitt
Deanne Buckingham
Deb Hayman
Deb Sytema
Deborah Tyler
Denomination Pty Ltd
Diana Rickard
Dimitrios Mouratidis
Don Ballantyne
Dwayne Charrington
Elizabeth Harrington
Elizabeth Minter
Elizabeth Schloeffel
Elizabeth Young
Emma Jones
Felix MacNeill
Fethon Naoum
Fiona McKinnon
Fiona Reynolds
Frances Parker
Gary Russell
Gaye Rutherford
Geoffrey Johnson
George and Kathy Deutsch
Georgina Costello
Gerard Abood
Gernot Keckeis
Gina Lyons
Godfrey van der Linden
Gordon Haywood
Greg Chapman
Gregory Moloney
H Kronberger
Heather Davey
Helen Mundy
Helen Stewart
Helen Sutherland
Peter & Gretta Carmody
Howard Williams
Ian Duncan
Ian Neil
Ingo Weber
Ivor Ries
Ivor Spillett
J Deane Miller
Jack Patton
Jackson Harding
Jacqueline Doon
Jacqui McDonnell
James M Swinton
James Mclachlan
James Paterson
Jan Browning
Jane Mussett
Janet Dean
Janet Kajons
Janet Shelley
Jean Wyldbore
Jean-Francois
Jeanette Rogers
Jeff Bezos
Jen Mitchell
Jennifer Gawne
Jennifer Paratz
Jeremy Wells
Jeta Vedi
Jock Given
John Bonnett
John Buckingham
John Connolly
John Firth
John Grigg
John Hinde
John Mather
John McGrath
John Nash
John O'Donovan
John Pratt
John Rouse
John Simpson
John van dde Rhee
Joseph Tan
Josephine Harrison-Cobby
Judith O'Byrne
Judith Phillips
Judith Whitworth
Julie Kimber
Karen Ashley
Katherine Parsissons
Kathleen Hughes
Kathy Humphrey
Kaye Hargreaves
Kelly Leydon
Keren Gould
Kim Nicholson
Kirrily C Whish
Kit Hauptmann
Lara Bailey
Leon
Leoni Mather
Lesley Branch
Liz Wilkinson
Lois Cooke
Louise Harrington
Lucy Adeney
Lyle Gurrin
Lyn Casey
Lyn Spillman
Lynda Stoner
Lynette Bicknell
Lynn Wood
Mardi Kristin Iversen
Margaret Pickup
Margaret Scanlon
Marilyn Brookes
Mark
Mat Fitzsimmons
Matthew Chinn
Meg Bowyer
Meg Paul
Melanie Simpson
Michael Benjamin
Michael Burkitt
Michael Denning
Michael Dunkel
Michael Jones
Michael Lord
Michael Pickering
Michael Wiggin
Michelle Trowse
Mike Armstrong
Molly Hanrahan
Monique Harrison
Mr.Russell Drysdale
Murray Roberts
Nada Kirkwood
Nancy Shearer
Nat
Natasha Baxter
Nathan Borgelt
Neal Ryan
Nicci Holland
Niti Saraf
Noel Richard Gilbert
Noeline Rudland
Owen Lock
P. Russell
P. Hutley
Paddy O'Toole
Pam O'Donnell
Patrea Ryan
Patricia Heaton
Patrick Norris
Paul Boxer
Paul Moneta
Paul Munro
Paul Spillane
Paul Waizer
Paul Werskey
Paul Wilson
Penny Wright
Peter Bowtell
Peter Dutton
Peter Laing
Peter Toohey
Peter Walsh
Philip Lloyd Henseleit
Phillip Haley
Phillip Moulds
R Madgwick
Rachel Edwards
Rae Mae Brokensha
Rebecca Lehman
Rebecca Whelan
Reda Saad
Richard & Amanda O'Brien
Richard Duckett
Richard Garside
Richard Johnston
Richard M Glover
Rob Giles
Rob Stack
Robert Pearce
Robert Thomas
Robin Bowles
Robyn Newton
Ron Grim
Rosamond Nutting
Rosemary Luke
Rosemary Nixon
Rosemary Peterson
Roslyn oRR
Ross Cayley
Ross Hosking
Sally Jackson
Sally Kirk
Sam Reale
Samuel Yates
Sandra Bird
Sandra Hodge
Sara Branch
Sarah Koops
Sarah Martin
Scott & Sharyn Zrna
Scott Morrison
Scott O'Keefe
Shane Smith
Shaun Norris
Sheila Mcmillan
Sheryl Aylward
Simon Pellatt
Stephanie Bennett
Stephen
Stephen Babyszka
Stephen Gateley
Steve Burns
Steven Durrington
Stewart Gillies
Sue Wareham
Susan Grace
Susan Provan
Tamara Shardlow
Terry Ledlin
Tiffany Venning
Tim Cherry
Tim Hannan
Timmy
Tom Evers
Tony Mclean
Trevor Hogan
Valerie
Vanessa Owen
Vanessa Petrie
Victor Moore
Victor Zbar
Victoria Taylor
Warwick Sherman
Wayne Morris
William Cluney
Yvonne D Cooke
Ziggy Costello
Zoe Probyn

2021 Review

powered by Google

Started out reasonably enough – received a warm welcome when we walked in. But then a horde of Neo-Nazi Americans dressed as Jamiroquai stormed the place, and it really set everything off wrong.

We asked to start off with a few Pfizers, which the waiter said would be out straight away. But they didn't end up arriving until three-quarters of the way through the night. Turns out the order was never put through to the kitchen. Amateur hour.

Things just got worse from there. The Afghan dish was totally abandoned, some old bloke stood up at the table next to us and announced to everyone that he hadn't done a shit in his pants, a group at the bar started doing shots of horse wormer, and some rich guy in a suit sued us for defamation.

In hindsight, we should've left when the music changed to Delta Goodrem. But some waitress wearing an employee-of-the-month gold star badge assured us it would turn off by itself. Well, it absolutely fucking didn't. She somehow managed to make it get even louder and then blamed us for not doing enough to turn it down.

Just as we were finishing up dessert the Pfizers finally came out, only to be given to a bunch of private school boys sitting at a table near the window. The group doing horse wormers turned up the music even more, the gold star waitress resigned mid-shift and the poo-in-his-pants guy started running around with a toy submarine. Then a manager named Dan threatened to call the cops if we didn't leave by 9pm.

Awful. Avoid.

The Shovel Annual is

Written by: James Schloeffel

With contributions from: Chris Auld, Matt Harvey, Joanna Jericho, David Trajanoski, Adam Reakes, Jess Nicholson, Niall Ginsbourg, Donald Mackay, Peter Tovey, Patrick Bruck, Ian Gason, Simon Matthews and Martin Welzel.

Layup by: Caz Smith

Edited by: Mum

Tonight I'll be eating

WHATEVER SCOTT MORRISON SAYS HE'S GOING TO EAT

Why The Shovel Was Awarded The Contract To Oversee Australia's Vaccination Rollout

It has recently been revealed that, in August last year, The Shovel was awarded a $400 million contract to oversee the rollout of Australia's COVID-19 vaccination program.

While this was intended to remain commercial-in-confidence, some irritating journalist, probably from the ABC, used a Freedom of Information request to release the details of the contract, and we've been inundated with angry emails ever since. This statement is designed to answer some of the most common questions.

How the fuck did a satirical news organisation get awarded the contract to oversee Australia's COVID-19 vaccine rollout?

A lot of people seem to be very angry about this, but we were just as entitled to apply for the contract as anyone else. It was a rigorous tender process, with several checks and balances along the way. The fact that one of our writers went to school with Greg Hunt and we donated $1.5 million to the Liberal Party last year is purely coincidental.

Does the Shovel have any experience managing vaccination programs?

No, but we did organise a very complex pub crawl for 80 people in 2012, which involved multiple venues, and several different brands of beer (some imported, some made here in Australia). So it's basically the same thing.

What? A pub crawl isn't like a vaccination rollout at all

Obviously you haven't seen our COVID-19 vaccination rollout yet.

Do you have any medical experience at all?

The morning after the pub crawl required a fair bit of medical ingenuity. But, apart from that, no. But what we lack in medical expertise we more than make up for in comedic ability.

What comedic skills could possibly be of use to a vaccination program?

Timing. Actually, no, bad example. We've totally fucked up the timing. But we have incorporated one of the other central tenets of comedy into the program – the element of surprise. GPs are constantly telling us how surprised they are when they receive eight vials of the vaccine rather than the 400 they had been promised.

This is a disaster, isn't it?

No, not at all. Everyone seems to be focusing on targets, but we put those in place purely for satirical purposes. I think we can all agree that setting a target of 4 million vaccinations by March, falling short by almost 3.5 million vaccinations, and then getting Greg Hunt to say "The national vaccination program is accelerating exactly as intended" has all the hallmarks of great satire. Although nitpickers would argue it was technically farce.

Is this the first time the government has awarded a commercial contract to a satirical organisation?

No, in 2019 the Government awarded News Corp $345,000 to set up a spelling bee website.

Has The Shovel been awarded any other government contracts?

Apart from a contract to run a series of empathy training courses, no.

A complete list of The Shovel's tweets that were read out in Senate Estimates in 2021

The Shovel
@TheShovel

Imagine being the chief law officer and fucking up your own defamation case. It'd be a bit like being the health minister and fucking up a major vaccine roll ... oh wait

4:55 PM · Jun 1, 2021 · Twitter Web App

3,397 Retweets **157** Quote Tweets **13.8K** Likes

Statement regarding Senator James Paterson's connection with *The Shovel*

15th June 2021

Last week Senator James Paterson used a Senate Estimates hearing to read out a popular tweet written by The Shovel.

The incident generated a significant amount of media coverage, with many people questioning why the Senator was spending his time looking through the tweets of a satirical news organisation, rather than doing his job as an elected official.

Given the interest in the matter, we felt it was time we came clean.

Mr Paterson is not a real person, but rather a satirical character created by The Shovel, initially as a joke, but more recently as a way of increasing the reach of our content.

We never really expected the prank to work. The idea of a man whose central belief is the minimisation of government, even though most of his career has been spent in taxpayer funded employment, did seem to be stretching believability somewhat. Plus, he looks about twelve (adult actors are expensive).

But the Liberal Party fell for it, they put him at the top of the Senate ticket and our guy somehow got elected.

We did consider pulling the stunt at that point. But after some consideration, we decided to lean into the project, giving him various tasks and media appearances where he would talk about wacky policy ideas that we'd made up over a few beers the day before. We even gave him a fake beard to try and increase his credibility.

Recently it began to occur to us that the character could be used, not just for our own amusement, but also as a way to increase the reach of The Shovel – particularly amongst the 80-85 year old demographic who watch Senate Estimates hearings.

And so last week we told him to start reading out our tweets. We were certain our cover would be blown at this point – a 33 year-old man spending his Saturday nights trawling through the Twitter accounts of ABC journalists just seemed so utterly unbelievable. But, unlike most things in Parliament House, it actually worked.

While the exposure has been great, we feel now is the right time to reveal the truth. We've run out of idiot policy ideas and 'Senator Paterson' is getting bored of going to Gina Rinehart's parties.

That said, we won't be retiring the character just yet. Despite the fact that he is now known to be fake, we expect him to be comfortably reinstated at the next election. After all, Scott Morrison is clearly the construct of an advertising agency brainstorming session, but people seem to love him.

How to ruin your career in 3 easy steps

By Christian Porter

Do you ever get the feeling that your career is going smoothly? Luckily, it's easy to fix.

You're earning $350k a year. You've been touted as the nation's next PM. And you seem to keep getting promoted for no reason. What a nightmare! Here's how to destroy it all in under 6 months.

Step 1: Cultivate a ludicrous level of self belief

An essential ingredient for the most dramatic career implosions is an unshakable belief that you're the smartest person in Australia. What you're after here is hubris so obvious it would make even an ancient Greek playwright blush. To get started, go to an elite private school in Perth, spend 20 years in the Liberal Party and you're on your way.

Step 2: Sue the national broadcaster

Some people like to pick a legal fight with a neighbour or a local business. But if you're serious about destroying everything, can I suggest suing a government-funded media organisation over an article that doesn't mention your name. To make it extra problematic, aim to do it while you're the nation's Attorney General. When you later pull the case and are left with eye-watering legal costs, claim it was a humiliating loss for the victor (see Step 1).

Step 3: Take donations from ISIS

Or the Chinese Communist Party, or Vladimir Putin or your local heroin importer. Who knows! I certainly don't. By setting up a $1 million blind trust and then casually listing it on the register of parliamentary interests as if you've been gifted a souvenir coffee mug, you'll be on your way out in no time.

SHOVEL DATA CENTRE

IN A PANDEMIC, INFORMATION IS CRITICAL. THE SHOVEL DATA CENTRE HAS BEEN RUNNING SINCE EARLY 2021 TO HELP REGULAR AUSTRALIANS MAKE SENSE OF THE BIG ISSUES.

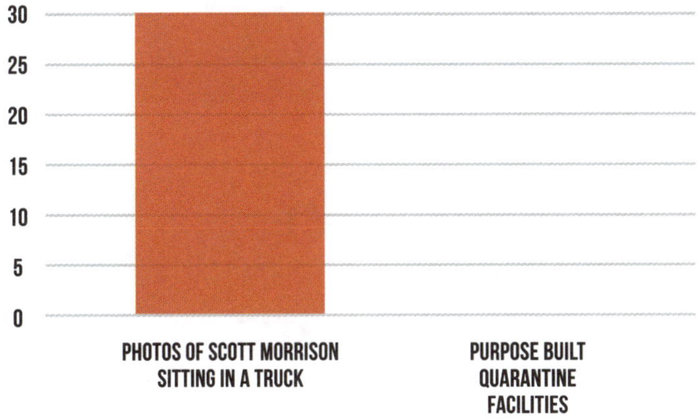

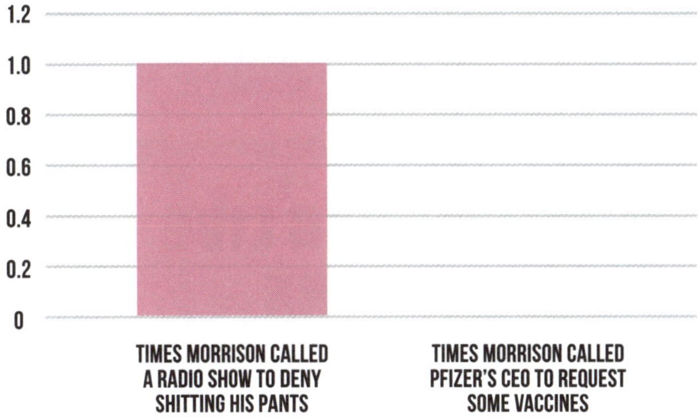

30
25
20
15
10
5
0

PHOTOS OF SCOTT MORRISON SITTING IN A TRUCK

PURPOSE BUILT QUARANTINE FACILITIES

1.2
1.0
0.8
0.6
0.4
0.2
0

TIMES MORRISON CALLED A RADIO SHOW TO DENY SHITTING HIS PANTS

TIMES MORRISON CALLED PFIZER'S CEO TO REQUEST SOME VACCINES

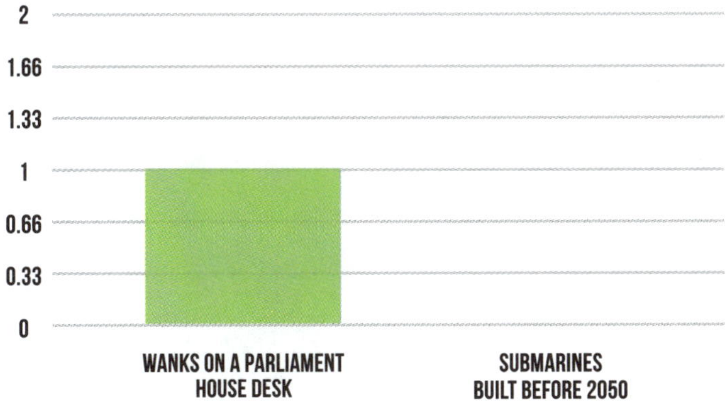

2
1.66
1.33
1
0.66
0.33
0

WANKS ON A PARLIAMENT HOUSE DESK

SUBMARINES BUILT BEFORE 2050

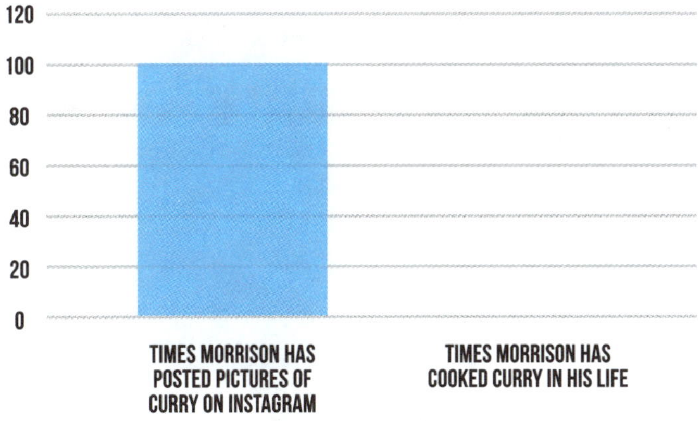

120
100
80
60
40
20
0

TIMES MORRISON HAS POSTED PICTURES OF CURRY ON INSTAGRAM

TIMES MORRISON HAS COOKED CURRY IN HIS LIFE

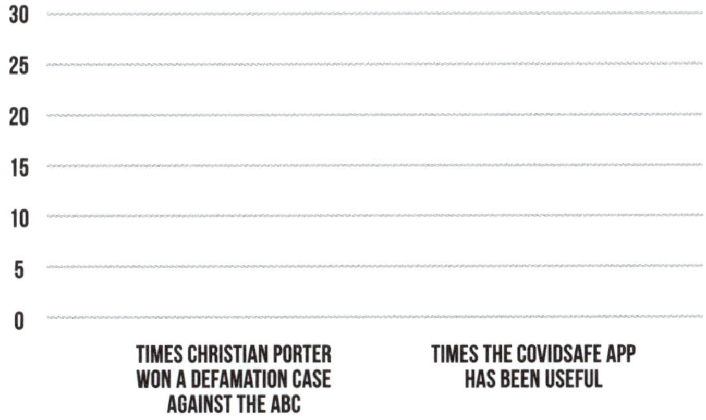

30
25
20
15
10
5
0

TIMES CHRISTIAN PORTER WON A DEFAMATION CASE AGAINST THE ABC

TIMES THE COVIDSAFE APP HAS BEEN USEFUL

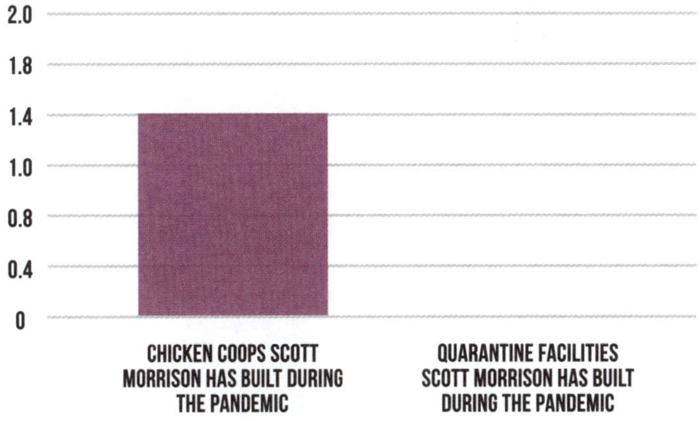

2.0
1.8
1.4
1.0
0.8
0.4
0

CHICKEN COOPS SCOTT MORRISON HAS BUILT DURING THE PANDEMIC

QUARANTINE FACILITIES SCOTT MORRISON HAS BUILT DURING THE PANDEMIC

TRACKING THE DEFAMATION ROLLOUT IN AUSTRALIA (%)

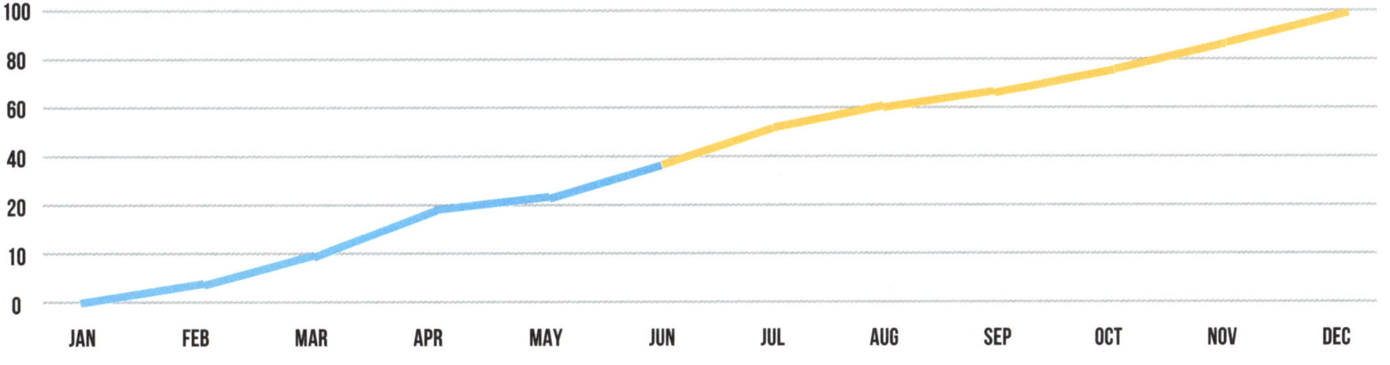

SCOTT MORRISON
A MAN OF HIS WORDS

When our Prime Minister says something, he means it. For a while. Until focus group testing tells him he should say something different. Then he'll say the exact opposite.

We've commemorated this rare oratory skill by combining two Morrison quotes into one succinct statement, so there can be no uncertainty about what he means.

"WE CAN LIVE WITH THE VIRUS WITHOUT LOCKING DOWN IS THE ONLY WAY OUT OF THIS"

"IT'S NOT A RACE. IT'S NOT A COMPETITION. IT'S ABOUT THE HEALTH AND SAFETY OF ALL AUSTRALIANS, LIKE OUR OLYMPIANS, ARE GOING FOR GOLD!"

"WE WILL GET ALL AUSTRALIANS VACCINATED BY OCTOBER AS WE ALWAYS SAID WE WOULD NEVER SET A TARGET FOR THIS VIRUS"

"CHRISTIAN PORTER REMAINS AN INNOCENT MAN AS FAR AS I'M CONCERNED IF SHE DOESN'T WANT TO STAND ASIDE, SHE CAN GO"

"I COMMEND PREMIER BEREJIKLIAN FOR NOT LOCKING DOWN SHOULD HAVE HAPPENED SOONER IN NSW"

"YOUNG PEOPLE SHOULD NOT TAKE ASTRAZENECA IS STRONGLY RECOMMENDED FOR EVERYONE"

"I TAKE THE ISSUE OF SEXUAL ASSAULT SERIOUSLY, HOW WAS I SUPPOSED TO KNOW THERE WAS A RAPE IN PARLIAMENT HOUSE?"

"WE HAVE NINETY NINE PERCENT EFFECTIVE QUARANTINE MANAGEMENT IS A MATTER FOR THE STATES"

Tonight, I'll be eating My own words

Uber Eats

Uber Eats

New Evidence Suggests COVID Vaccine May Have Originated In A Lab

Morrison Becomes Longest Serving Liberal PM Since Peta Credlin

Woman Achieves 427-Day Streak Of Not Logging Into Duolingo

Morrison Dismisses Claim He Is NSW Centric, Saying He Governs For All 8.1 Million Australians

An angry Scott Morrison has hit back at the Victorian Government's claims that he gives special treatment to New South Wales, saying he works tirelessly for each and every one of Australia's 8.16 million citizens.

Wearing a Sharks scarf and a Blues cap, Mr Morrison said he was offended by the notion that he only looked after his own.

"I don't care where you're from – I really don't. Whether you're from somewhere in the south of the country like Cronulla, or up north in Avalon I am your Prime Minister. Whether you're from Bondi in Sydney, or all the way out in Penrith in Western Australia, I work for you.

He said his job meant he had the opportunity to see parts of the nation he had previously not visited. "Like North Ryde. Previously I'd only ever been to Ryde".

Asked whether he had plans to visit Melbourne, the PM said he would go there as soon as international borders re-open.

Government Launches New Track & Trace App, To Find Out What Happened To COVIDSafe App

The Federal Government has announced plans for a new $80 million track and trace app to discover the whereabouts of the COVIDSafe App, which hasn't been seen since April 2020.

The new app – officially named WhatTheFuckHappenedToCOVIDSafe – will use sophisticated tracing technology to pinpoint any member of the federal government who has come within a mile of COVIDSafe within the last eighteen months.

"It's a bit like finding a needle in a haystack. No-one seems to have been willing to go anywhere near it," the app's lead developer Rebecca Luton said.

"We know, for example, the Prime Minister hasn't come within a mile of the app since last April. But there must be someone who has had some sort of contact with it, even briefly".

Luton said one of the problems with traditional contact tracing was that people often don't want to talk about sensitive or personal details. "People don't want to tell us embarrassing things like totally ballsing up what was supposed to be the central component of Australia's coronavirus response. But with this new app, we're confident we'll be able to track down what's happened".

The new app will initially only work on Nokia 5110 phones and will be launched with a $750 billion advertising campaign. Plans are already in place to develop a new app to find this latest one, once it also goes missing.

Britney Spears's Dad To Take Control Of Australia's Vaccine Rollout, After Government Found Unfit To Manage Own Affairs

"We Have Secured An Additional 10 Million Announcements" Morrison Confirms

The Morrison Government has secured a further 10 million empty announcements, which will be rolled out over the course of 2021.

"That brings us to a total of 150 million largely meaningless, but highly effective media announcements in total," the Prime Minister said.

The 10 million new announcements, announced today, are in addition to the initial 10 million announcements, announced last year.

Health Minister Greg Hunt said Australians wanted certainty in the nation's announcement rollout. "As we've announced before, we will begin by rolling out 80,000 announcements a week, and then look to accelerate the rate of announcements as they become announceable".

The announcements announced today are a highly effective form of announcement, proven to be at least 95% effective at distracting attention away from less announceable announcements. "In many cases it eliminates the bad news altogether," the Prime Minister said.

A further 50 million less effective announcements will be used when the other announcements run out.

Couple Who Work At Google Already Finishing Each Other's Sentences

A couple who have been dating since they met at a Google office party last month are already finishing each other's sentences, it has been revealed.

"It's so cute. I'll say something like 'What is ...' and then Jack will say 'Dwayne Johnson's net worth'. He knows exactly what I'm going to say, sometimes before I do," account manager Freya Campbell said.

"Or the other day I just said 'Can you ...' and he immediately said 'overdose on Panadol' which is not what I was going to say, but then he said 'eat green potatoes'. So he got it second go".

Jack Greenberg, 26, said the two already know each other intimately. "We know what each other's thinking. Often very specifically. This morning I said, 'How do you ...' and Freya said 'say hello in Spanish/ get shingles/know if a girl likes you/ make pancakes'. All things I had been meaning to ask. Uncanny".

A friend of the couple said the two are very cute together. "The other day in the staff kitchen Jack said, 'How do I ...' and Freya said 'know if I'm pregnant?' And that's how we found out. Adorable".

Trump Leaves Poignant Letter For Biden, Reminding Him That His Ratings On The Apprentice Were Very, Very High

Keeping with the tradition started by Ronald Regan, and continued by Presidents Bush, Clinton, Bush Jnr and Obama, Donald Trump has left a letter for his successor, using the opportunity to remind the incoming president that The Apprentice received some of the highest ratings we've seen in a very long time.

Trump's letter, which he left for Biden in the Oval Office, read:

Dear Joe,

When I walked into this office just now, I was reminded again of the amazing ratings my television show received between 2004 and 2015. They were very, very high. It was incredible. A lot of smart people watched it.

You will be President when you read this note. But it is unlikely that you will have your own successful TV show on a major network. I did for many years. It is still incredibly popular.

It is the highest honour for an American citizen to receive six, sometimes seven million viewers per week. It is something I can be very proud of.

There will be trying times for you over the coming years. But when things get tough, just remember that in one particular episode – the season finale in 2004 I think it was – there were over 20 million viewers. That is a very big number.

Yours,

Donald J Trump

Australia Agrees To Send Troops To Support America's Invasion Of America

Citing the two nations' close friendship, and Australia's long history of supporting American military interventions, Scott Morrison has told Donald Trump that Australia will provide immediate support for America in its war against arch-enemy America.

"I didn't even let him finish his sentence," Mr Morrison told journalists today. "Donald said he was planning to go to war, and I said, 'You don't even need to tell me who it's with, we're there with you. Just tell us what you need and it's yours.

"That's what mates do. We were there shoulder-to-shoulder in Bagdad, we were there shoulder-to-shoulder in Kabul, and we'll be there in – sorry just checking my notes here – we'll be there in Washington DC too".

Critics were quick to denounce the plan, saying it was yet another example of Australia signing up to a war it couldn't win.

"Once again, we're off to help the US invade a poor, dysfunctional nation with huge oil reserves, without any plan for rebuilding it later," one foreign analyst said."

Australia will send 500 troops who will be stationed in a small shopping mall in New Hampshire.

Australians Planning Copycat Movement To Take Over Capital Chuck It In After Realising They'd Have To Go To Canberra

A group of activists looking to mimic the events in the US by storming Parliament House have pulled the plug, after someone pointed out it would mean going to Canberra.

"I'm all for taking back our country and freedom and that, but you gotta draw the line somewhere," activist Rob McManus said.

"We were all fired up and ready to cause some mayhem. And then Johnno told us that Parliament House was in Canberra, and we said nah, stuff that. Where are we going to celebrate afterwards? Mooseheads?".

Co-conspirator Jason Black said he never would have got involved in the plan had he known where Australia's capital was. "I went to Canberra for a school excursion in 1997 and it was boring as fuck. I'm a patriot, but everyone's got limits".

Black said another member of the group did push ahead with the plan to drive out to Canberra. "But then he hit the first roundabout, took a wrong turn and ended up in Jindabyne".

We've got some great

JOBKEEPER SAVINGS!

CONSCIENCE CLEARANCE SALE, ALL ETHICS MUST GO!

$22 MILLION
CONSEQUENCE FREE

NO SHITS GIVEN

NO INTEREST IN PAYING IT ALL BACK

We make massive fucking profits, take handouts from taxpayers and don't pay our staff properly. Fun!

Come in and buy an overpriced fridge today.

Absolutely no conditions apply. Although we reserve the right to have a massive fucking whinge at short notice about competitors who use the internet to sell things.

WANT TO PAY 3x MORE FOR THE SAME PRODUCT YOU'D FIND ON AMAZON?

Visit **Harvey Norman .com**

This tiny text is so small you hopefully won't even read it.

A Statement About Our Donation To Christian Porter's Blind Trust

19th September

Well, that turned out well. A few weeks back we decided to transfer $1 million into the blind trust we'd set up for Christian Porter. Yesterday he resigned. We'll be honest, we didn't expect it to work quite so quickly.

After all, you have to clear a pretty high bar to get sacked from a Scott Morrison cabinet. An accusation of sexual assault won't do it. Cocking up a vaccine rollout in a pandemic won't do it. Allegedly doctoring documents to discredit the Sydney Lord Mayor won't do it (actually, that will get you a promotion).

But, as we now know, receiving money from a satirical organisation is where the line is drawn. The truth is, Christian Porter actually knew all along that a satirical news service was funding his defence. But he thought it was Sky News, not us, which is why he went along with it. Whoops!

Australian comedy, as you all know, is incredibly lucrative. But even for us, a million dollars was a large sum. So thanks to everyone who has chipped in as a supporter over the years. I think you'll agree, it was well worth it.

The Shovel

The Shovel

Victorians Stuck In NSW Have Had Plenty Of Time To Become Professional Tennis Players, Premier Andrews Says

Victorians complaining about being stranded in New South Wales due to the hard border closure have only themselves to blame, Daniel Andrew says, pointing out they have had weeks to qualify for the Australian Open.

"Victorians have known for a long time now that the quickest way into the state is via a top 150 ATP tour ranking. It's a bit rich now to say that you haven't been hitting enough balls or playing enough satellite tournaments to get your ranking up. What have you been doing with your time?"

He said qualifying for the grand slam event wasn't the only way into the state. "You could become a professional coach, or an ATP or WTA official. You could become a family member of a top player. Or a major event sponsor. There are hundreds of ways. I feel like I'm stating the obvious sometimes".

Encouragingly for those trapped away from home, officials have confirmed that there are still wild card qualifying spots up for grabs in the Open.

"Facts Are Contentious" Says Former Heroin Addict Michael McCormack

Bidgee/Wikipedia

"Facts are contentious and what you think is right, somebody else might think is completely untrue," the Deputy Prime Minister, who depending on your version of events may or may not have resorted to prostitution in the late 1990s in order to fund a heroin addiction, said today.

Mr McCormack, who some claim murdered a man during a robbery gone wrong, said the truth was up to the individual. "It's not the government's role to stop misinformation," he said, refusing to comment on allegations of sexual assault in his office, which could be true or totally made up.

The Nationals leader, who according to certain versions of the facts, is having an extra-marital affair with the husband of one of his junior staffers, said he didn't believe in fact-checking.

Hunt Thought Email From Pfizer Labelled "Life-Changing Drug That Will End Pandemic" Was Spam

Responding to revelations he took two months to follow up on a meeting request with the pharmaceutical giant, Mr Hunt said the email seemed a little bit fishy.

"The email came into my inbox, I saw that it was spruiking some sort of life-saving treatment or mRNA technology or some such, which all seemed very dubious, and so I marked it as junk, as any conscientious health minister would. I thought they were trying to sell me something.".

He said he junked a second email from the company a week later. "The second one seemed even more urgent, saying things like 'last chance!', 'don't miss out!' and 'order now or risk looking like an incompetent idiot as you lead your country into an entirely avoidable third wave of the pandemic'. I mean, who would believe that?"

Hunt said the fact that the company followed up with eighteen phone calls, four text messages and a personally signed letter from the Pfizer CEO didn't change his mind. "These scammers can be very sophisticated in the way they use your personal details," he said.

TRADE WAR: Kmart Retaliates By Pulling All Chinese-Made Goods From Its Shelves

Kmart says it will do its bit to support Australia in the escalating trade war with China, committing to remove all Chinese-made items from its stores.

A spokesperson for the company said it was an important symbolic gesture. "It's something small we can do to show our support. We started by removing any clothing made in China, then homewares, sheets and towels, electrical appliances, toys, underwear, maternity wear, belts, hats and sporting goods. Then we moved to Christmas decorations, books, nappies, pet items, handbags, footwear, stationery, swimwear and sleepwear.

"From there it was just a matter of removing the shelves, the light globes, the flooring, the shopping trolleys and the curtains on the change rooms and we were done. You can hardly notice any difference at all".

He said there was still a great range of items in store. "All of the self-serve checkouts were made in Japan. So, come in and take a look".

Kmart rejected claims it had put all of its eggs in one basket. "Our baskets are actually made in China, so no, we haven't put anything in a basket".

CAN YOU GET SACKED FROM THE MORRISON GOVERNMENT?

START HERE!

YOU RORT TRAVEL EXPENSES

OOPS! PAY IT BACK
THEN HAVE ANOTHER TURN

YOU PAY 10 TIMES TOO MUCH FOR LAND

LUCKY IT WASN'T YOUR MONEY
WAIT HERE FOR KICKBACKS

YOUR ROBODEBT PLAN IS ILLEGAL

GOOD THING YOU'RE
NOW PRIME MINISTER
COLLECT $500K

YOU REFUSE TO GIVE EVIDENCE IN AN AFP PROBE

YOU'RE PROMOTED TO
ATTOURNEY GENERAL
ADVANCE 1 SPACE

YOU ACCEPT $1 MILLION IN A BLIND TRUST FROM SOMEONE YOU DON'T KNOW

MINOR SETBACK!
GO BACK 2 SPACES

AUSTRALIA'S MOST DIFFICULT BOARD GAME!

YOU FORGET TO BUY VACCINES IN A PANDEMIC!

BLAME SOMEONE ELSE
GO FORWARD ONE SPACE

SICK LEAVE

WAIT HERE INDEFINITELY

YOU CALL SOMEONE A LYING COW

THAT'S TERRIBLE!
TAKE 5 WEEKS OFF THEN ADVANCE 1 SPACE

COMPULSORY EMPATHY TRAINING

MISS 8 TURNS
AND COLLECT $200K

YOU FORGE A DOCUMENT TO DISCREDIT AN OPPONENT

AT LEAST IT WASN'T $80 MILL WORTH OF WATER
GO BACK 4 SPACES

YOU'RE SACKED!

ENJOY YOUR CUSHY NEW PRIVATE SECTOR JOB

FEBRUARY

Search For Anthony Albanese Continues

Govt Strikes Deal With Facebook To Restore News. Also Facebook Now Owns Tasmania.

Most Typing Errors Caused By AutoCock, Research Finds

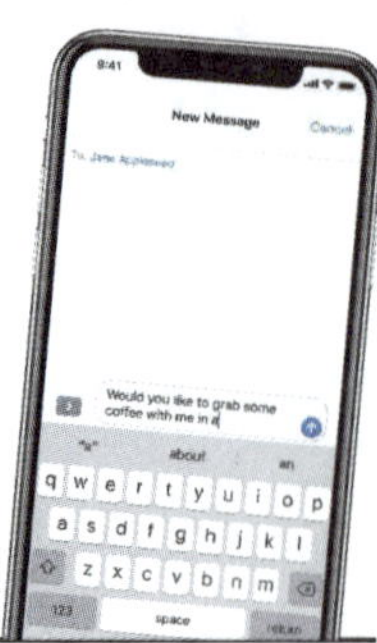

Eddie McGuire Dismisses Racism Claims: "One Of Our AFLW Players Has An Asian Friend"

Collingwood President Eddie McGuire has denied his club has a racism problem, pointing to dozens of examples of diversity at all levels of the club.

"We have a girl in the AFLW team whose best friend is Asian - they've been friends since primary school. One of our club physios learnt Indonesian at high school, to quite an advanced level I'm told. And not one, but two of our under 19s players travelled extensively through Africa on a gap year before joining the club. So don't tell me we have a problem with racism," a furious McGuire said.

Pushed further by journalists to provide examples of how the club was addressing racism, McGuire said the VFL team held their 2019 end of year trip in Thailand. "And I don't want to tell you how to suck eggs, but that's in Asia mate," he said.

McGuire said the club had a proud history of inclusion and equal rights. "From day one we've been committed to setting aside 50% of our jumper for non-white colours. Some people might call that affirmative action, but I call that inclusion. You won't find any other club doing that," he said.

Flickerd / Wikipedia

NSW Residents Facing Fourth "Once In A Hundred Year" Event Since Last January

As flood waters continue to rise across the state, residents of New South Wales are weathering their fourth once-in-a-lifetime event since the start of last year.

Penrith resident Helen McMannis said she would be telling the grandkids about the floods of 2021, after she'd finished telling them about the floods, smoke, bushfires and global pandemic of 2020.

"I haven't seen a weather event of this scale during a Sydney summer since last summer," she said.

Jude Johnson, whose property was burnt down last year before being covered with a dust storm, then flooded, then overtaken by mice, said his street was underwater yesterday.

"I remember the last once-in-a-hundred year event like it was just last year. You won't see something as bad as this again, until something worse comes along in a few months," he said.

Doctor administering vaccine reassures Morrison he's just a little prick

AAP / DARREN PATEMAN

Mum Lets Little Boy Sit In Rocket Ship At Shopping Centre

A 52 year-old little boy has been allowed to have a turn sitting in the rocket fighter ship outside Coles, after his Mum couldn't put up with his whinging anymore.

"One turn and then that's it," his mother said, hoping that three minutes in an imaginary aeroplane would be enough to satisfy the boy's need to act out his little fantasies.

"No, sorry, you'll have to just pretend to shoot down all the poor people," she said, confirming that she would not put a coin in the slot to make the space missile laser ship go around and around and around.

"Pew! Pew!" the little boy said, as his mother reminded him that he had one more minute and then they had to go home to have a bath and dinner.

Initially refusing to end his turn, the boy finally agreed to get off if his mother organised a team of professional photographers to mark the occasion.

Jeff Bezos Steps Down From Amazon, Citing Appalling Working Conditions

Daniel Oberhaus, 2019

Amazon CEO Jeff Bezos has handed in his resignation, saying he can no longer withstand the horrific working conditions at the company.

Bezos, who has worked at the company for almost 30 years, said enough was enough. "The pay is ok, but the work is absolutely demoralising. Yesterday I had to piss in a bottle because the company doesn't allow bathroom breaks. Some of the staff here wear diapers for god's sake!"

He said staff were held to impossible standards. "We get a 15-minute break each day, but the break room is a 15-minute walk away! Whoever runs this place is a maniac.

"People here are pushed to the limit, all just so that some chump in Minnesota can get his toaster delivered same day. I'm not a robot. I'm a person".

The Amazon board said Bezos would be replaced by a cheaper, more efficient automated CEO.

Scott Morrison Agrees To Properly Fund Education After Jen Tells Him His Daughters Go To School

The Prime Minister has agreed to increase funding to Year 7 and Year 9 classes after his wife reminded him he has daughters who attend school.

Mr Morrison said he had never thought about education policy before, but was now totally committed to the cause.

"We were sitting down to dinner last night and I mentioned that I was looking forward to totally gutting the education system, and then Jen says 'but our daughters go to school'. And I said 'shit I totally forgot. Not just about the school, but about the daughters'.

"And so I asked the kids what year they were in at school and I immediately called the education minister and said 'let's federally fund Years 7 and 9.' It was a no brainer.

"It's just so important that we take education in these specific years seriously. After all, I know what it's like to have a daughter in Year 7 or 9".

Asked if he would also consider increasing funding to tertiary education, a confused Mr Morrison said the kids weren't at uni yet. "I don't have a daughter at university, so I don't understand what you mean, sorry".

Jobseeker Increase Means Recipients Can Now Afford To Rent An Apartment In Sydney In 1994

The announcement of a $3.47-a-day increase in the JobSeeker allowance has been met with jubilation by people across Australia, who say they will now have the funds to rent a rundown flat in outer Sydney 25 years ago.

The weekly payment now totals $307, enough to easily feed and house a family of four before the turn of the century.

"I kinda don't know what I'm going to do with all the extra cash," one JobSeeker recipient said today. "With $25 extra a week I'll be able to fill up the car with petrol, in 1983".

DFAT / WIKIPEDIA

Scott Morrison Says He Wasn't Aware Of Most Recent Rape Allegations Until February 2024

The Prime Minister says he wasn't made aware of the new allegations of sexual assault at Parliament House until after the next Federal election.

Questioned in Parliament today, Mr Morrison said he would ask the secretary of his department to double check the dates in question, but repeated that he personally had no knowledge of the reports during this term of government.

"I am disappointed that no-one will tell me about this for the next three years, but until they do, there is really very little I can do about it, I'm afraid," he said.

Morrison assured the Parliament that he would act on the allegations as soon as he is made aware of them. "The minute I am told about this latest sexual assault I will immediately sit down with my wife to understand if I should take it seriously or not".

The Prime Minister agreed to launch an investigation into why his office didn't know about the claims. The investigation will be run by the Prime Minister.

Prime Minister's Office To Take Urgent Action Against New Sexual Assault Allegations: "We'll Start Work On Discrediting The Woman's Family Members Immediately"

With a fourth woman coming forward to say she was raped at Parliament House, a staffer within the Prime Minister's Office said the issue had the office's full attention.

"When you hear about something as serious as this, your immediate reaction is, what can we do to help? Is there a boyfriend we can get some dirt on? A family member perhaps? Can we reframe this as someone else's fault? If there's anything at all we can do to change the narrative and put the blame back on the victim, then let's do that straight away".

The staffer said helping to undermine a sexual assault victim was a natural human response. "You just want to do what you can to help".

Christian Porter Agrees To Meet With March4Justice Organisers If They'll Iron His Shirt First

'You Just Don't Know What's In Vaccines', Says Man Who Eats Meat Pie For Lunch Every Day

Morrison Checks With Wife To Determine If Wanking On Desks Is Appropriate

Australia To Take Stress Leave From Government

Australia has announced it requires eight-weeks paid mental health leave to deal with the absolute clusterfuck of a government running the country right now.

A spokesperson for the Australian people said it was distressing to have to watch on while the government tried to cover up a rape allegation, bully the victim, intimidate her family, then abolish the family court, pivot seamlessly to side-stepping another rape allegation, hijack International Women's Day, cock up the vaccination roll-out, abuse a rape victim again and then have an MP admit to taking weird photos of women.

"And that's just this week. It's too much. We will be going on a short period of leave to assess and hopefully improve our mental health".

The Prime Minister was asked to comment on the nation's decision but was unavailable due to being on leave.

IKEA Renames Its 3-Seat Sofa 'The WA Liberal Party' To Commemorate Historic Election Result

Swedish furniture giant IKEA has re-named its VILME 3-seat sofa 'The Western Australia Liberal Party' in recognition of the party's remarkable election achievement.

A spokesperson for the company said they were always looking to celebrate novel approaches. "And winning just three seats at a state election is certainly novel".

She said the company had sent one of the newly-named sofas to Liberal Party HQ. "It's big enough to hold full party meetings. We've also sent them an armchair for shadow cabinet meetings".

A Liberal Party strategist said he didn't want to underestimate the task ahead. "We've just been sent a few cushions, an Allen key and some planks of wood. The rebuilding task is going to be significant".

Man Who Remembers Bowl Of Prawns From 1988 Doesn't Know Who Put $1 Million In His Bank Account

House Floating Down Sydney Street Sells For $3 Million Above Reserve

An un-renovated terrace in Marrickville (at the time of writing) has sold for $3 million over its reserve.

Billed as having good bones with plenty of scope for improvement (STCA), the three-bedroom home was said to be in need of a new kitchen and bathroom, as well as new foundations and land.

"You won't find a 3-bedroom terrace in Sydney for less than this," real estate agent Hugo Tarnby told bidders, as they swam to keep up with the property.

The home, which started in the sought-after suburb of Enmore, before floating to Marrickville and then Tempe, was at times close to shops, public transport and other amenities.

"It's close to everything, eventually," Tarnby said. "It has 360 degree absolute waterfront views. Don't let this one pass you by. And I mean that very literally".

Successful bidders Jo Granton and Jeremy Peach said they were ecstatic to finally get onto the property ladder. "It's not perfect, but it's got great potential. Of course we would've loved a house that was connected to the ground, but this is Sydney! You can't have everything."

Welfare Recipient Down To His Last 193 Department Stores

A man who is dependent on government payments for his livelihood has literally less than 200 electrical, furniture and bedding retail stores to his name.

The 81 year-old battler, who can barely afford to buy basics such as racehorses without the help of government payments, says if things don't get better soon he may be forced to make a derogatory statement about homeless people.

"A lot of people don't know what it's like to live year to year, not knowing where your next $22 million cheque from the government is going to come from. If it wasn't for those payments, I'd be left with literally just tens of millions of dollars. It's heart-breaking".

The Sydney man, who some have described as a welfare sucking leech, said he didn't know where he was going to sleep tonight. "I've only got 12,000 different beds to sleep on, and they've all got to go!"

ELEVEN QUOTES FROM THE BIBLE

THAT BACK UP SCOTT MORRISON'S CLAIM HE'S 'DOING GOD'S WORK'

A video emerged this year of the Prime Minister claiming he's been called upon to 'do God's work'. But is he really carrying out the work of the Almighty Father? It turns out, yes. We've uncovered eleven quotes from the Bible that substantiate Mr Morrison's claim.

John 12:16 – And the people said unto the Lord 'Why hath we no immunisations?' And the Lord said unto them, 'That is a matter for the states'.

Luke: 5:21 – Jesus looked at the poor and the helpless and the needy, and he said unto them, 'Unfortunately I have no money to give you because I gave $4.6 billion in taxpayer money to companies that didn't need it'.

Romans: 8:33 – And John, who was one of the Lord's 40 media managers, said to Jesus, 'Lord, your poll numbers are down. Let's set up a photo shoot of you building a cubby house for chickens'.

Matthew 25:35 – For I was hungry and you gave me something to eat, I was thirsty and you gave me something to drink, I was a stranger and you locked me up in an island prison for an unspecified amount of time.

John 11:18 – Jesus said, 'Send me your sinners and lepers and Robodebt collectors. Especially your Robodebt collectors'.

Mark 8:17 – The people suffered through the worst pandemic in a hundred years. And Jesus went to Bunnings.

James 2:8 – And Matthew, one of the Lord's disciples, said, 'God's love is for everyone. But especially for those living in marginal Liberal electorates'.

Luke: 2:12 – The fire burnt for 40 days and 40 nights. And Jesus hopped on the first flight to Hawaii.

Corinthians 6:21 – Peter, Jesus' disciple, didn't like the mean things people said about him. So he sued for defamation.

Matthew 4:1-25 – Then Jesus was led up by the Spirit into the wilderness to be tempted by the devil. And after fasting forty days and forty nights, he was hungry. And God came and said to him, "It's a bit like that movie The Croods".

Mathew 13:47-50 – Jesus told the people the parable of the three workers. The first worker called a rape victim a 'lying cow', but she kept her job because the government had only a one-seat majority. The second worker took a photo of a woman's underwear, but he kept his job and was sent on an empathy training course. The third worker gave her staff Cartier watches, "And if she does not wish to stand aside, she can go!"

Potato Threatens To Sue For Defamation Over 'Insulting' Comparisons To Peter Dutton

A creme gold potato says it will start suing social media users if that's what it takes to stop the defamatory comparisons to Immigration Minister Peter Dutton.

"I'm sick of it, to be frank," the potato said in an interview with radio station 2GB. "Every single day I wake up to see these very insulting comparisons, often with an image of me side by side with Peter Dutton, and it's quite distressing. I've had enough".

The potato said it was tired of being roasted. "I don't even see the likeness. Well ok, I do, but that's not the point. The point is it's not my fault that I look like this. How would you like it if every time you went out for a drink people said 'Oh look, that potato totally looks like Peter Dutton. It's a slur, and I won't take it anymore".

The potato urged listeners to live a day in his skin. "I'm just a regular vegetable trying to do my job and yet I'm being compared to someone who locks up kids. Well I'm sorry but I'm not going to put my head in the dirt anymore. I'm not a monster. I'm a potato".

banger1977 / Flickr

Urgent Desire To Shop At Kmart And Bunnings Confirmed As Covid-19 Symptom

An uncontrollable desire to travel across town to visit as many Kmart and Bunnings outlets in a 48-hour period as possible has been added to a loss of smell, fever and a dry cough as key signs of COVID-19.

"We've analysed hundreds of positive COVID-19 cases and what we've found in the vast majority is that, in the days leading up to a positive test, the person in question has found themselves frantically shopping for affordable homewares and hardware," a scientist on the study said.

"In many cases there seems to be a compulsion to travel to multiple stores, often across a large geographic area".

She said theories were beginning to emerge as to why the strange behaviour occurred in COVID-positive patients.

"We believe the purchase of DIY materials or a great-value set of cushions may be the brain subconsciously preparing for 14 days in lockdown".

Authorities have acted quickly on the findings, urging anyone who finds themselves going to more than one Kmart in a day to get tested.

"If you find yourself madly travelling across the city to shop for discount hardware and soft furnishings, please – get tested immediately".

Nation 'At Front Of Queue' Discovers It Is In Wrong Queue

Prince Philip Died 12 Years Ago, Coroner Confirms

Anti-Lockdown Protesters To Be Sent To Afghanistan To Compare 'Dictatorships'

Making Inappropriate Jokes Is What Prince Philip Would Have Wanted

Making slightly off jokes about a person's appearance and background is exactly what the late Prince Philip would have wanted, aides have confirmed.

"He always had that way of making you feel just a little bit awkward," said a friend, noting the Prince had officially died yesterday, but looked as if he had died over a decade ago.

"If he were here today, he would have made a joke, or at the very least said something racist.

"He had a sense of occasion. It was in the most serious of moments – moments such as these – that the Prince always had a way of finding just the wrong words.

"Sure, many of his jokes didn't age well. But then neither did he".

Prince Philip Died Because Meghan Markle Murdered Him, Daily Mail Reports

Prince Philip died because that scheming American actress who tore apart the monarchy killed him, tabloid news outlet The Daily Mail is reporting.

According to the Daily Mail's exclusive sources, the Prince's life was cut short when the American actress spent time at Buckingham Palace this week. "She was in the kitchen holding a large knife and looking very mixed race and the next thing you know the Prince is dead," the source said.

"Or maybe she was cutting up carrots and the Prince had a heart attack – it's impossible to say. But what is absolutely true is that she was wearing an ugly dress when it happened, and it looks like she's put on weight too".

Man Who Had Brief Conversation With Prince Philip In 1964 Interviewed For Half An Hour By ABC

Man Brings Book To Bed So It Can Sit Next To Him While He Looks At Phone

Self-described 'book lover' Jeremy Randle took a novel with him to bed last night, so it could sit on his bedside table while he scrolled through his phone for 2.5 hours.

The Sydney man said he had planned to read the first chapter of the book, but thought he should check his phone first just to make sure he hadn't missed anything important. "I hadn't. But now it's 2:30 in the morning and I need to sleep".

He said it was nice to surround yourself with books. "I think it's important to have a house filled with books that you pretend you're going to read.

"Right now I'm not reading Jane Austen. But last year I was really into almost reading George Orwell. He's got such great book covers".

Government In Talks With Essendon To Learn How To Successfully Roll Out Injection Program

Health Minister Greg Hunt will meet with members of the Essendon Football Club next week, hoping to gain tips on how to successfully inject a large group of people quickly and effectively.

"One of the differences I've noticed between their injection program of a few years back and our vaccination program now is that they didn't talk about it at all and yet managed to inject all of their playing group within a day, whereas we talk about our program non-stop but haven't managed to inject anyone.

"I'm hoping they'll come on board to manage the program actually, because they seemed to get 100% compliance. Not a single complaint. So I'll be asking about that as well"

Morrison Solves Quarantine Debacle With $600 Million Gas Plant

Government Announces Budget Surplus Of Negative $161 Billion

COVIDSafe App Identifies Outbreak At Cedar Meats In 2020

Totally Fucking Up Immunisation Rollout Was Part Of God's Plan, Morrison Says

Making a total balls-up of a vaccination rollout in the middle of a global pandemic while offloading every other responsibility to state governments was how Jesus would have done it, the Prime Minister says, reiterating that he is just doing God's work.

"I am carrying out God's plan. And, funnily enough, his plan was for me to monumentally botch this whole thing, even though I only had one job," the PM said.

"When every other country was out there in May last year eagerly buying up every different vaccination, God said to me, 'Nah, it's better if you wait a few months until you miss out on the first round of orders, buy up just a few vaccines, and then just tell everyone back home that they're first in line'. So that's why we are where we are".

While some people were surprised that God had chosen a failed sales rep to carry out his work in Australia rather than a miracle-working prophet, or at the very least a qualified professional, Mr Morrison said he was just doing what he was told.

"If you're unhappy with the rollout then, I'm sorry, but don't complain to me, complain to God. I'm just working through him. Not my responsibility".

THE SHOVEL NEWS IN BRIEF

MAY

Morrison Secures 100,000 Additional Photo Opps To Help With Victorian Outbreak

New Homeopathic Treatment Significantly Reduces Levels Of Cash In Your Wallet, Study Finds

India Changes Name To 'Aspen' To Enable Australian Citizens To Return Home

Australians stranded in India will now be able to return home, after the Asian nation temporarily changed its official name to 'Aspen, Colorado'. Those returning from 'Aspen' will not be required to quarantine.

"When there's a humanitarian crisis, we like to try and help out where we can," a spokesperson for the Aspen Government said. "We realise the word 'India' is a little confronting for some Australians, so we changed it to the name of a more palatable COVID disaster zone".

Some Australian-Indians are not taking any chances, choosing to also change their own names to help smooth the process at Australian airports. 'Kerry Stokes', formally Ishaan Patel, told immigration officials he is looking forward to returning to his job as a 'French au pair' in Brisbane. "They organised a limo for me from the airport".

Rahul Chakrabarti, who now goes by the name 'Novak Djokovic', said he also had no issues passing through immigration.

Prince Harry Releases New Book, Podcast, Movie Franchise In Desperate Bid For Privacy

Prince Harry has signed a new 82-part tell-all reality TV documentary series in a desperate plea for privacy, reminding fans that he also has a new Netflix special and book series in the works.

"This constant interest in my day-to-day life has to stop. It's like living in The Truman Show," Prince Harry told viewers of a prime-time talk show, which he used to promote a new upcoming movie.

"All I ask is that you stop this fascination with my personal life and subscribe to my new podcast, wherever you normally get your podcasts".

The Prince said the last few years had been incredibly trying and that tickets to his new live show would be on sale soon. "Meghan and I just want to get on with our lives, which you can view on our new reality TV show, starting next month. Check local guides for details".

Frydenberg Starts Budget Speech With Reminder That All Figures Are Correct To Closest $60 Billion

Bill And Melinda Gates's Marriage Has Encountered A Problem And Needs To Close

Bill and Melinda Gates have announced that they will be shutting down their marriage, after other attempts to keep it working failed.

In a joint statement, the couple of 27 years blamed busy lives. "We have had too many applications open at once".

The couple - one of the richest in the world – said they had worked hard on their marriage, turning it off and then on again several times. "No matter what we did, we couldn't seem to open up for each other".

Despite the shock news, Melinda Gates was philosophical about the end of her marriage of nearly three decades: "When one window closes, another one opens. And then all the windows you had open inexplicably close, you lose a day's work and you get asked if you'd like to send an error report".

Neither Bill nor Melinda has announced whether they will be upgrading, although Bill has assured his former wife he is not a browser.

Whoops! Anti-Lockdown Protesters Fighting For Human Rights Forget To Attend Rally For Asylum Seekers

Thousands of anti-lockdown protestors took to the streets in Melbourne again last night, claiming that they were there to fight for everyone's human rights. But in an embarrassing oversight, all of them forgot to join any one of dozens of rallies held in recent years for asylum seekers locked in detention.

"There I was shouting 'Freedom!' and 'Don't lock people up!' and 'Give us back our human rights!' And then all of a sudden it occurred to me that I've never ever stood up for anyone else's human rights before. It's almost as if it was all about me," one protester said.

Another protester said she had intended to go to a rally in support of the rights of asylum seekers, Palestinians or other neglected groups, but totally forgot. "It's been busy. I've been so focused on my fundamental human right not to put a piece of cloth on my face that I just totally forgot to think about people getting shot at."

She said she now remembered that she had a lot in common with asylum seekers. "I've been confined to just my house and my local park, café, Bunnings, Coles and Woolworths since July, so I know what it's like to be locked behind bars on a small island for seven years."

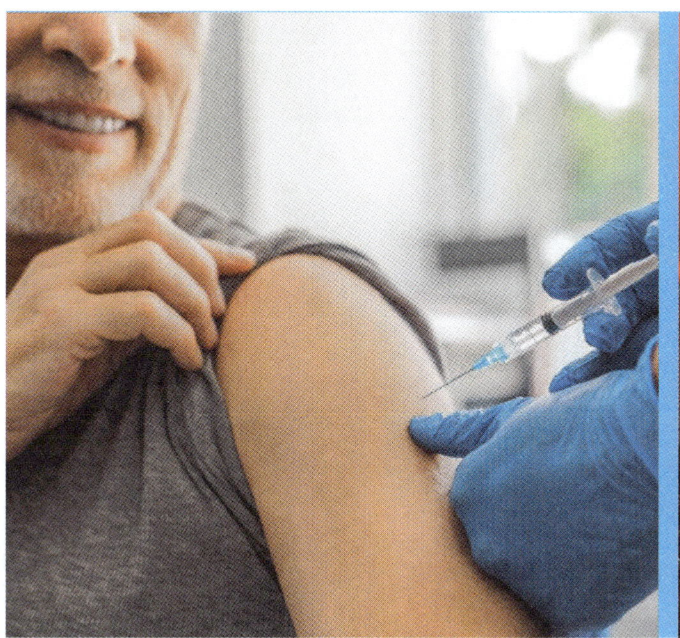

Government Launches 'No-Jab-No-Negative-Gearing' In Desperate Bid To Increase Take-Up

With a concerning number of Australians saying they will hold off on getting immunised, the Morrison government has announced a new policy that will require people to get vaccinated before they can write off their investment property. The policy is expected to increase take-up of the vaccine to 100%.

Health expert Riley Dimitreou said if there was one thing that older Australians feared more than an AstraZeneca vaccine it was missing out on middle-class welfare. "We're confident that any complaints about 'personal freedoms' or 'needing more data before I'm convinced' will dissipate immediately once people realise their tax rebates are at risk".

Barbara Henning, 70, who owns three investment properties and claimed last week she was 'concerned about contracting autism' now says she is totally comfortable getting the jab. "I was very worried about it. But then I heard I might be forced to pay a fair rate of tax and all of a sudden I found myself lining up to get a vaccination. The science is pretty clear on this stuff. I'm not sure what all the fuss has been about".

This Morning's Coffee To Sell For Between $1 and $1.20 Barista Tells Real Estate Agent

A small flat white is expected to fetch north of $1, a real estate agent was told at his local café this morning.

The coffee – which eventually changed hands for $3.80 – went well above the quoted price, but was a reflection of market conditions, the café's owner said.

"We were surprised by the strong interest in this coffee. It certainly surpassed our expectations," owner Mark Crawford said.

The real estate agent said he was caught unawares. "I only came here with $1.50 to spend –a good 20% above the upper end of the quote range, so I'm guttered that I've walked out of here today without a flat white".

Man On Depressurising Plane Refuses To Wear Oxygen Mask Because It Breaches His Human Rights

Scott Morrison Running 20 Years Late For G7 Climate Meeting

Nation Relieved "Barnaby Spill" Refers To Leadership, Not Bodily Fluids

Joe Rogan Back To Full Health

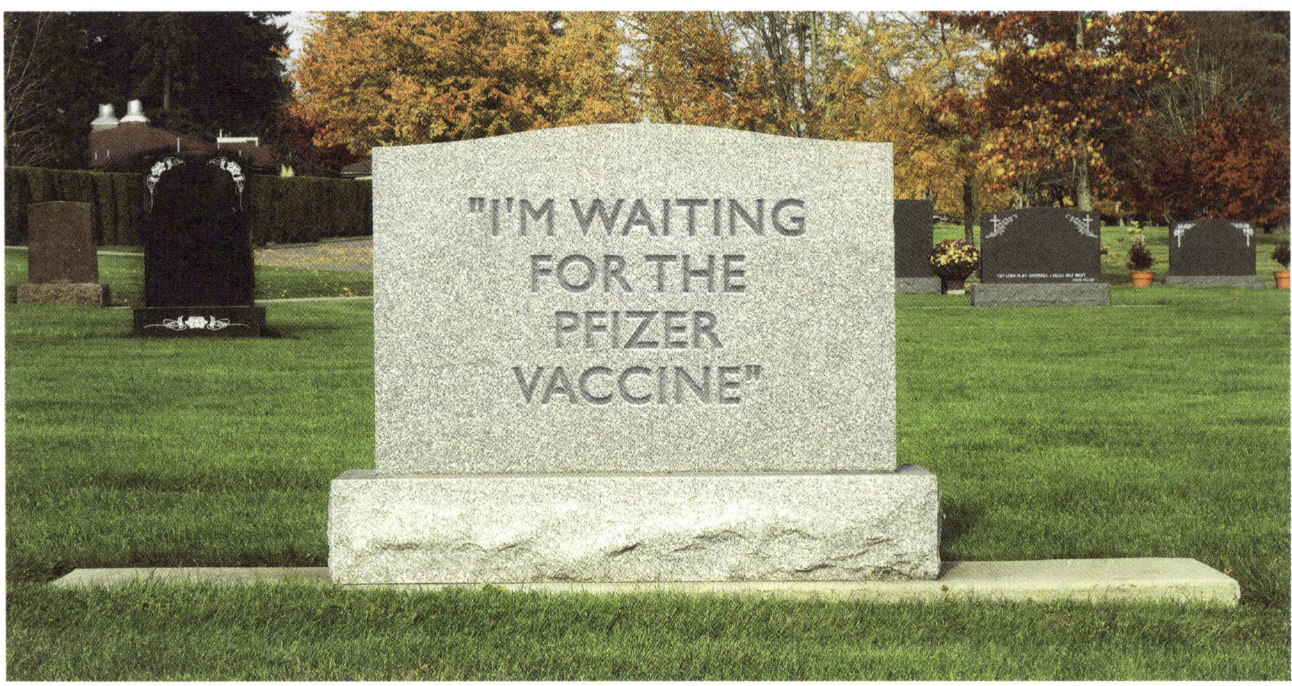

'I'm Waiting For Pfizer' Gravestones Now Available In Australia

A gorgeous new range of gravestones, engraved with the epithet 'I'm Waiting For The Pfizer Vaccine', has become available for Australians who have decided the currently-available vaccines aren't good enough for them.

A spokesman for Aussies Gravestones said Australians should have choice when it comes to their gravestone.

"We know there are lots of Australians who think getting a vaccine is like choosing from a wine list. Well, we want them to have that choice with their gravestone too".

The gravestones come in a range of different colours and sizes, with other phrases, such as 'I'll get a vaccine when I need to travel overseas again' and 'Barbara on Facebook said the vaccine wasn't safe', also available.

"What better way to capture someone's last words than on a tastefully designed marble headstone".

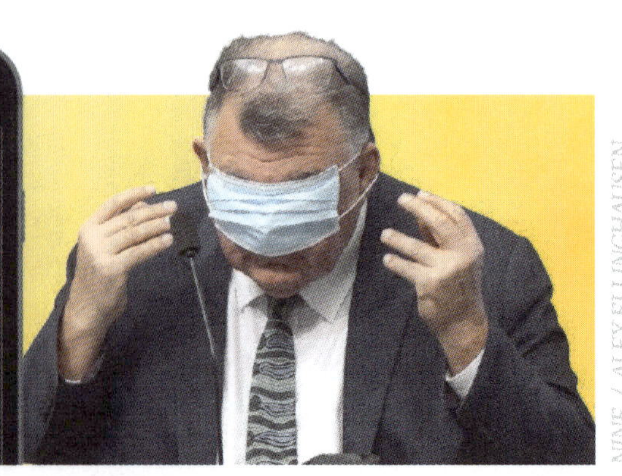

NINE / ALEX ELLINGHAUSEN

Barnaby Joyce Appointed To Status Of Women Taskforce. Says He Hopes Current Status Is "Single"

We Want To Be Careful Not To Reveal This Person's Identity, But A Senior Government Minister Has Massively Fucked Up His Own Defamation Case

Without disclosing information that might lead people to piece together the identity of the person in question, The Shovel can reveal today that a senior minister of the Morrison government is alleged to have thoroughly and utterly ballsed up a defamation case he (or she) brought against the ABC.

The MP is said to be a member of the Coalition, narrowing it down to one of only 180 Coalition MPs who have launched defamation proceedings this year.

The Coalition MP was educated at a private school, was in a debating team and is white. So no clues there.

But we can reveal that the man (or woman, it could be a woman) is believed to have held a senior ministry (ok, it's probably not a woman), possibly one relating to the legal profession. I mean imagine being the nation's chief legal officer and comprehensively fucking up your own legal action! Allegedly.

The MP has strenuously denied the alleged failure, saying the ABC was left humiliated after being told it would no longer need to defend an action it did not initiate.

Password Must Include At Least One Shakespearean Sonnet You Haven't Used Before

Your new password must include the full text of one of Shakespeare's sonnets, plus at least 48 characters from three different alphabets.

Bear in mind that you cannot use a Shakespearean sonnet that you have used in a previous password and you must include at least three numbers and no more than eight, but at least six upper case letters.

Sonnet 41 is not a valid password.

Users are reminded that explanation marks can no longer be used in passwords and must be replaced by the % symbol. The word 'love' is also deemed a security risk and must now be replaced with an open and closed bracket. For example "O% learn to read what silent () hath writ%".

Try to avoid passwords that can be easily guessed, such as Sonnet 18, which is pretty obvious.

The words 'thee', 'night', 'friend', 'summer' and 'sun' are prohibited.

Adding the lyrics of an early 90s Wu Tang Clan song is recommended, as long as they follow the form of an iambic pentameter.

Remember, never write down your password, or tell it to anyone else.

Thank you for signing up to Pete's Petfood Warehouse.

L32007 / Wikipedia

New Four Corners Episode To Explore PM's Links To Crazy Conspiracy Group

The ABC's Four Corners will go ahead with an episode examining the Prime Minister's connections to a strange conspiracy group that believes there is an invisible being in the sky who hates gay people and knows when you're having a wank.

The bizarre conspiracy alleges that a 'judgement day' will come when non-believers will be rounded up and thrown into a pit of fire. To avoid the fire, believers must perform specific rituals and make shit-tonnes of money.

It is alleged that the Prime Minister is well connected within the conspiracy sect, even inviting a senior member of the sect to an official meeting in Washington DC.

The group, who often communicates by speaking a made-up, childlike language, is an offshoot of a larger group which believes a woman who had never had sex gave birth to a boy who could walk on water.

It is also alleged the Prime Minister may have links to QAnon.

Scott Morrison Too Lazy To Be Part Of QAnon

AAP Image/Mick Tsikas

The Prime Minister doesn't have the work ethic to be part of a complex conspiracy network, it has been revealed.

Experts say the requirement to constantly keep up-to-date on new information and be across the latest 'drops', is not in keeping with the Prime Minister's preference for doing absolutely nothing, all of the time.

"It's a lovely theory, but it's just not true," one conspiracy expert said.

"Have you ever looked at a QAnon chatboard? It's exhausting. The energy required to keep up with that shit is well beyond Scott Morrison".

She said the sheer complexity of the conspiracy theory counted Morrison out. "It's possible he's outsourced his belief in QAnon to a staffer. But I think it's unlikely he's actually doing anything himself".

Scott Morrison strenuously denied links to the QAnon conspiracy, saying he would never align himself with such a movement, unless of course focus group research showed it was popular, in which case he would immediately claim to be a long-term believer.

38

Weather in Sydney today: Fine and 17 degrees. (3 of those degrees we already knew about and 4 degrees will be reported as part of tomorrow's forecast). So it's actually 10 degrees. Or 24. Maybe.

"Qantas Unaware Of Bikie Infiltration" Alan 'Mad-Dog' Joyce Says, Before Announcing New All-Leather Uniform

Recent intelligence reports suggesting that organised crime groups had infiltrated Qantas are untrue, CEO Alan Joyce - who asked to be addressed as 'Mad-Dog' - told a media conference today.

Joyce was forced to answer questions about the allegations at the media conference, which was originally called to launch a sleek new leather jacket addition to Qantas uniforms.

"These allegations are false," Mr Joyce said, itching his face where a new teardrop tattoo had been freshly inked.

"Qantas has some of the strictest background checks of any Australian airline, and I have every confidence in my newly appointed HR managers, Jimmy One-Eye, Mudpig and Brick, to see that appropriate care is taken reviewing our personnel files for any discrepancies."

When asked by one reporter if Qantas shareholders would approve of this increased spending during the COVID-19 pandemic, Joyce flicked his cigarette butt at their chest before referring any further questions to his assistant, Hamish 'The Hammer' Wilson.

Royal News: Man Just Assumes 'Lilibet' Is Name Of New Sports Betting Company

A man punting on the dogs at a local pub is unaware that Lilibet is the name of Harry and Meghan's new child and not a new online gambling company.

Richie Brackworth from Sydney said he'd been hearing a lot about this new Lilibet thing recently, but was frustrated when he was unable to find the app on his phone.

"I've got Sportsbet, Pointsbet, GoBet, WinnersBet, PalmerBet, BlueBet, Bet365 and UniBet ... but I'm not seeing Lilibet," he said.

"I was hoping to get an introductory bonus bet for race 6 at Sandown, but all I'm getting is pictures of some princess in America. Strange launch strategy".

Harry and Meghan launched their second child this week.

They have not ruled out selling the naming rights to a betting company.

Australia Swamped By People Wanting To Be Tortured On Small Island For Three Years

Thousands of asylum seekers have packed up their things and are headed for Australia after the Government announced it would allow the Biloela family to temporarily reunite in Perth after three years locked in a cage on a small island.

The move angered hardliners within the Government, who said there would be consequences for compassion. "This was a test of our nerve and we blinked," one MP said.

"Now everyone is going to think that all they have to do to get into this country is spend 1,000 days locked up on an island without any social interaction, and then wait for their child to contract a life-threatening blood disease. Talk about rolling out the welcome mat."

Ted86 / Wikipedia

Labor Promises To Torture Asylum Seekers More Humanely If Elected

Opposition Leader Anthony Albanese has launched a scathing criticism of the Government's treatment of the Biloela family, saying a Labor government would take a more compassionate approach to torturing asylum seekers.

"A lot of people say Labor's policy on asylum seekers is exactly the same as the Coalition's. That's simply not true. This government has held an innocent family in detention for two years on an island, without any social interaction or hope of release.

"Under a Labor government, this family would have been held for two years on an island without any social interaction or hope of release, except we'd change the name to 'processing' rather than 'detention'. It couldn't be more different".

He said the majority of Australians wanted to see a more humane approach to asylum seeker policy. "What the Coalition government is basically saying to desperate people is, 'Don't come here or we'll torture you'. It should be 'Don't come here please or we'll torture you'. Manners don't cost anything".

Fuck, This Guy Again

'Here we fucking go again', the nation has sighed, following the announcement that a drunk, shouty, dog-murdering Kiwi in an Akubra has re-emerged as the second most powerful person in the country.

"Lock up your small dogs and update your employee relationships policies, Barnaby is back," a spokesperson for the nation said.

"Just when I'd managed to erase from my memory the image of a sweaty Barnaby Joyce having sex in his office with a staffer while wearing nothing but his RM Williams, here he is again ready to tell me all about it.

"Guaranteed by the end of the day we'll have a press release, a double-page feature article and a TV special with Barnaby giving us an update, then telling us he wants us out of his private life.

"It's only a matter of time before we get some phone-video rant saying he wants the government out of his life, forgetting he literally is the government.

"And I guess now he'll start his tour across the country lecturing us about family values while having an affair. It's all so absolutely exhausting."

Berejiklian Announces Sydney Lockdown Area To Be Extended To Include Entire Country

Sydney's lockdown area will be extended to include the outer Sydney suburbs of Perth, Melbourne, Darwin and Brisbane, the NSW Premier has confirmed.

In an emergency press briefing this morning, Ms Berejiklian said she had made the difficult decision to push the existing Blue Mountains boundary a further 3,500 km west. The lockdown in Sydney's northern beaches will now extend to Noosa.

"This lockdown now includes all of the Greater Sydney area – from Bondi to Cottesloe," the Premier said. "We need to do this for the rest of the country".

Asked if the restrictions would also extend to Adelaide and Hobart, Ms Berejiklian said she wasn't aware of those suburbs.

Ben Roberts-Smith To Use 3-Month Adjournment To Find New And Peculiar Ways To Ruin His Reputation

With the defamation trial he initiated now adjourned until November, former SAS solider Ben Roberts-Smith says he will use the valuable time off to find interesting new ways to undermine his reputation.

"I'm not sure I've done enough to taint my character, so it'll be nice to have a few months to focus on that," Roberts-Smith said today, while drinking his morning coffee out of a prosthetic limb.

He said he didn't want to waste the time just lazing about. "I could use the spare time kicking back watching the Olympics. But why do that when I could place my laptop in an oversized lunch box and bury it in the backyard?"

He said he wanted to use the time productively, not just lying around scrolling through his phone. "I find the best way to cut back on phone usage is to seal your phone in a plastic bag, set it on fire and then throw it into a lake. Your screen time drops immediately".

AstraZeneca Now Recommended For Anyone Who Has The Remotest Idea Of What The Fuck Is Going On

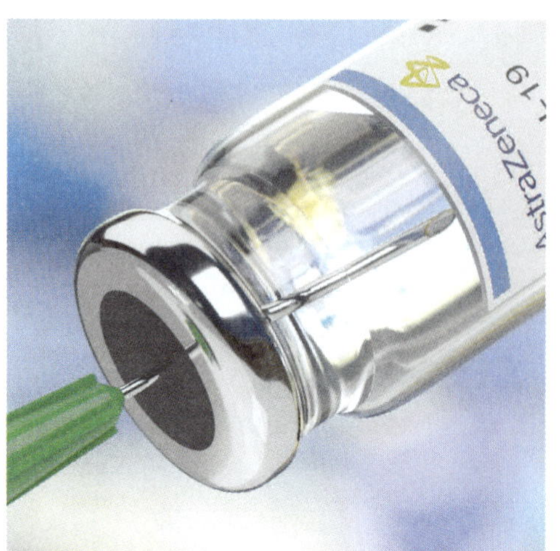

In new advice released today, the Government says that the AstraZeneca jab is now recommended for anyone who can even vaguely keep up with the latest policy on the rollout.

In a media conference today, Health Minister Greg Hunt said the government's advice was clear. "The AstraZeneca vaccine is open to all 25 million Australians, as long as they are over 60 but not younger than 70, or any age over 18 but born in March of a leap year, except 1974.

"That was yesterday's advice of course. But now we are saying it is open to anyone who can decipher what the actual fuck I am saying on any given day, subject of course to supply constraints. It really couldn't be any more straightforward".

Mr Hunt said the Government simply followed the medical advice, except on the days when it didn't. "We take what the medical authorities tell us, we mix it with some polling data and then place it into one of those big Powerball machines, give it a spin and then pick out a policy. I really can't understand why the take-up hasn't been higher".

'Do I Need To Wear A Mask While Doing Lines Of Coke?'

And 9 Other Questions From Sydney's Eastern Suburbs

With Sydney's Eastern suburbs the first to face the state's restrictions, we've collated some of the most common questions about the new rules

Distancing

Do I need to keep a 1.5 metre distance between my Porsche Cayenne and the Range Rover Vogue next to me in the supermarket carpark, or can I just be a fuckwit and park across two spaces as usual?

QR Codes

Whenever I go to check in at my day spa with my phone, my phone's camera is always pointing back at me (I think I permanently changed the setting ages ago). Do I show the person at reception the selfie I took, or should I just upload it to Instagram with a #Covidlyfe hashtag?

Masks

Are masks required while doing lines of coke outside, or just while in homes and offices?

Panic buying

In amongst all the craziness, we bought three investment properties last week. Are there likely to be per-customer limits introduced?

Police powers

How much is the fine if your mask doesn't match your activewear? If I see a crime being committed should I report it to the police?

Tests

I've heard COVID tests involve putting something up your nose. Can I just pay in cash when I get there or should I consult my dealer directly?

Symptoms

What are the first signs that house prices are about to drop?

Differing Viewpoints

I understand there are a lot of different views and we need to be open to all of them. But can we all agree that the window table at Icebergs on a Saturday afternoon is the best?

Density limits

How many litres of lip filler can I have per square centimetre?

Exceptions

My Mum is desperately sick and lives in Britain. Can I still go to Port Douglas for a girls' weekend next month?

Victoria Bans Nazi Symbols, Sky News Shifts All Filming To Sydney

Kevin Rudd In Talks With Kleenex CEO To Secure 10 Million More Bog Rolls

Morrison Government Commits To Zero Admissions By 2022

"Australians On Track To The Path Leading To The Bridge That's Heading In The Direction Of The Road To Normalcy" Announces Morrison

Calling it a 'new deal' for Australia's response to the COVID-19 pandemic, Prime Minister Scott Morrison has outlined the roadmap for Australia's pathway to the journey towards our passage that will take us to the finish line.

"We now have a map to get us to the four-stage horizon pathway," Mr Morrison announced, being careful to point out that he doesn't actually hold the map.

"While we don't know how long it will take to get there, or how we will get there, or where we will get to when we get there, or why we're going, or when we'll leave, or who will be coming with us, Australians should feel reassured knowing that, after 17 months, we now have a clear course towards the highway horizon outcome. I won't be taking any questions. Thank you".

The new approach will begin at some point in the future and has already started. It is subject to change.

THE SHOVEL
NEWS IN BRIEF

JULY
Daniel Andrews Refuses To Scrap 9pm Curfew But Agrees To Let Melburnians Read In Bed Until 9:30

Matt Canavan First Person Over 5 To Throw Temper Tantrum About The Wiggles

Man Announces 4-Phase Pathway For Paying His Taxes

A Sydney man has informed the Government that he will be paying his income tax based on a 4-Phase Allocation Horizon.

Outlining the new approach today, 28 year-old Josh Banister said there were no dates or figures attached to the payment rollout, but they may be added if and when appropriate.

"This is a New Deal between me and the Australian Tax Office," Banister said.

"Phase 1 of the pathway is to make an announcement about the pathway," he said, confirming that he was now in Phase 1.

"Phase 2 is when I start talking about paying taxes. Phase 3 is when I start preparing my tax forms. And Phase 4 is when I actually pay the tax".

He said there was no timeline determining how quickly he would move through the phases. "Right now we're in Phase 1, so I really can't comment on anything else until we move into Phase 2. That could be in a month's time, it could be in a year's time.

"What I don't appreciate is this pressure from the Tax Office to impose times and dates on the pathway. What is this obsession with targets? I will move through the Phases as and when it is appropriate".

Jeff Bezos Relishes New Opportunity To Look Down On His Workers

Fulfilling a longtime dream, Amazon founder and world's richest man Jeff Bezos said his 10 minute sub-orbital journey today gave him a totally new way of looking down on his company's workers.

"They seem so tiny and insignificant," Bezos said of his workers last year. But the flight on his Blue Origin rocket gave him a different perspective. "To look down on them from 100km in the air made what has always been metaphorical for me, a reality," he said.

Bezos said he was awestruck by just how inconsequential Amazon staff were. "They're like little ants, all scurrying around doing what they're told. At least that's what I used to think. But from up here it's clear they're much more trivial than that".

In an attempt to make the Blue Origin experience feel more like an Amazon workplace, passengers were not able to take a bathroom break during the flight.

Kevin Rudd, Harold Holt, And 4 Other Former Prime Ministers Who Are Doing More Than Scott Morrison Right Now

We learnt this week that, in the absence of a full time Prime Minister, Kevin Rudd has been hitting the phones with Pfizer, to try to sort out Australia's vaccine debacle.

But it turns out Kevin isn't the only former Prime Minister doing more work than Scott Morrison right now.

HAROLD HOLT

Harold Holt went missing in 1967 while swimming near Portsea. He now works part time at a surf shop in Los Angeles. With a public swimming pool bearing his name in Melbourne, Holt provides at least one more community service than Scott Morrison.

BOB HAWKE

Bob Hawke died in 2019. But with his face now adorning a beer label, Australians are statistically more likely to see Bob Hawke in public than Scott Morrison.

PETA CREDLIN

Peta Credlin was Prime Minister from 2013-2015. Always the workaholic, she now has a full-time role promoting government policy on Sky News, and a part time role undermining Victoria's COVID-19 lockdowns.

SIR EDMUND BARTON

Currently residing as a statue in Port Macquarie, Australia's first Prime Minister is significantly more useful than Scott Morrison. He provides a small amount of shade, a place for pigeons to sit, and can be easily located, even in a crisis.

TONY ABBOTT

Tony Abbott works full time reminding Australians that, no matter how bad Scott Morrison is, he's not as bad as Tony Abbott. This role is currently up for review.

Image courtesy Blue Mountains Library

New Government Ad Tells Australians To Imagine Vaccination Is Like A Milkshake

The Federal Government has finally released a COVID-19 vaccination campaign. Launching the ad, Health Minister Greg Hunt said, "We asked ourselves, 'what could we do to make this absolute mess of a rollout even more confusing for the Australian public?' And then someone said, 'Let's use the analogy of a flavoured milk drink'. I think we all knew then and there that we'd nailed it".

[VACCINATION AD | SCN. 1]

SET: 50s Diner for unexplained reason

[Actor 1]: "Do you want to try a milkshake?"

[Actor 2]: "Yes I do!"

[Actor 1]: "Sorry, we didn't order enough milkshakes".

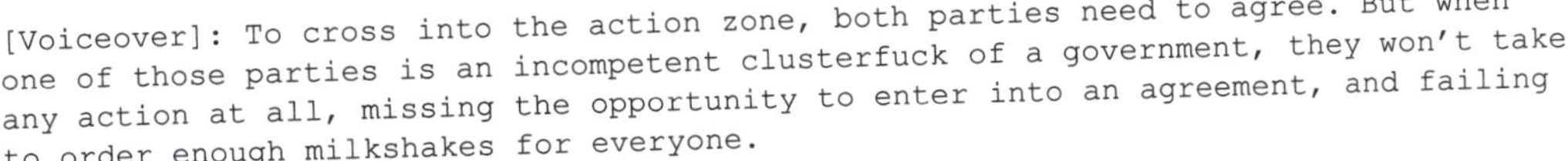

[Voiceover]: To cross into the action zone, both parties need to agree. But when one of those parties is an incompetent clusterfuck of a government, they won't take any action at all, missing the opportunity to enter into an agreement, and failing to order enough milkshakes for everyone.

[Actor 2]: "But I really want a milkshake".

[Actor 1] "You're under 40, sorry champ, you can't get a milkshake".

[Actor 2]: "But you told me I was first in line"

[Voiceover]: This is what we call 'moving the line'. A tricky technique where we give the impression that we're busy doing stuff, when in actual fact, we're doing absolutely nothing at all. Often that means totally dazzling you with announcements and photo opportunities and graphics with lots of milkshakes with our logo on it, moving the yes line over the maybe line and into the end zone. Whatever the fuck that means.

[Actor 2]: "I'm really angry at you right now".

[Actor 1]: "It's just a funny game, mate. Don't take it so seriously".

[Actor 2]: "But everyone else in the world is getting milkshakes".

[Actor 1]: "And if you were over 40 you'd be able to get a milkshake too".

[Voiceover]: Although if you were over 50, it wouldn't be the milkshake you want, because we've spent the last six months telling you it's a shit milkshake, and then telling you you need to drink it anyway.

[Actor 2]: "But it's not my fault I'm not over 40".

[Actor 1]: "Actually it is"

[Voiceover]: Actually, it is. Because one of the things we're very, very good at, is totally fucking something up, and then making it sound like it's someone else's fault. It's called not taking responsibility.

[Actor 2]: "But I go to a private school in Sydney".

[Actor 1]: "Oh. Really? Why didn't you say so? Well then of course you can have a milkshake. What flavour would you like?"

[1]

Morrison Offers Condolences To Aussies In Lockdown: 'I Know What It's Like To Do Absolutely Fucking Nothing'

Scott Morrison has offered words of support to those dealing with lockdown, saying he knows what it's like to do absolutely nothing at all.

In a Facebook video this afternoon, Mr Morrison said he stood with everyone in New South Wales, and was also aware of people in Victoria.

"To those of you not able to turn up to work, I know what it's like. I haven't turned up to work since 2008.

"To those of you who can't tick off that to-do list this weekend anymore, I'm with you. Although I find it's generally easier to not have a to-do list in the first place and then you won't be held accountable when things don't get done.

"To those of you who have no idea what you're going to do, neither do I. And that's got nothing to do with lockdown".

AAP IMAGES / MICK TSIKAS

THE SHOVEL NEWS IN BRIEF

AUGUST
Government Declare Pandemic Officially Over After COVIDSafe App Records 500th Consecutive Day Of Zero Cases

---

Mark McGowan Promises To Re-Open WA Border Once 180% Of Population Jabbed

Western Australia premier Mark McGowen has softened his stance on his state's border, saying he will consider opening up once 180% of the population is fully vaccinated.

"I've always said we'll take a common-sense approach to opening up," McGowen told journalists today. "Whether it's 180% or 190% we'll wait to see what the modelling shows us. But it's certainly something we're looking at".

He said it would be foolish to re-open at a 170% vaccination rate, as some in Western Australia have been advocating. "Look, I know there are some cowboys out there who are talking about those kinds of rates. But that would be reckless. We don't want to lose what we've got here".

A survey of Western Australia residents found that many believed the 170% rate was too cavalier. "There's still a risk," one said. But most said they were confident that dad would get it right.

Morrison Meets With Advisers To See If Vaccine Can Be Delivered Using Existing Copper Network

Gladys Asks Virus To Use Common Sense And Not Transmit To Others

NSW Premier Gladys Berejiklian has urged the COVID-19 virus to take a common-sense approach to the pandemic and not infect people within the community unless absolutely necessary.

Speaking directly to the virus at today's press conference, Ms Berejiklian said it was about doing the right thing and taking personal responsibility.

"We're not going to be providing a long list of the people you can and can't infect. What we're asking you is to think carefully before you go out – 'do I really need to infect this person today?' I think if we can take that common-sense approach and do the right thing, then we'll find our way out of this".

The Premier was hesitant to introduce a blanket rule about infecting and not infecting. "It is so, so hard to have a precise rule on this. That would lead to chaos. What we're saying instead is, exercise good judgement. If you can avoid infecting someone in New South Wales, please do so".

Sportsbet Ad Constantly Interrupted By Football Game

A 3-hour advertisement informing viewers of the latest sports betting odds has been annoyingly interrupted by a game of football, angry fans have revealed.

The Sportsbet presenter, who was giving a rundown of head-to-head, multi, first goal and best-on-ground odds, was forced on several occasions to stop mid-way through his spiel to cut to the game.

The disruption angered many fans who said they just wanted to sit back and be persuaded into handing over their money, without having to be rudely interrupted with snippets of football.

"It just wrecked the flow," one fan said. "One minute I'm learning about the head-to-head odds for Richmond v Carlton, and then all of a sudden they're talking about some live game of football. So annoying".

How to Look Busy While **Doing Fuck All**

By Scott Morrison

One of the things I've learned since being in the top job is that Aussies love a do-er. Someone who rolls their sleeves up, gets their hands dirty and chips in to get the job done. Sounds like a lot of hard work if you ask me.

Much better to just give the impression you're working, and then get paid half a mil a year to do sweet FA. Here are a few tips I asked my secretary to type up.

1. Go overboard on photo opps

Nothing says 'busy' like a professionally-styled photograph of a 55 year-old man doing barre at a meat processing plant.

If you think you've done too many cheesy photo shoots of yourself playing rugby on an 8-metre earth mover or hammering a nail into a F-15 fighter jet, then you haven't done nearly enough.

2. Put on a hard hat

There isn't a single situation where a florescent yellow hard hat can't make you look like you're a dedicated, untiring workhorse.

Signing a document you haven't read? Put on a hard hat. Heading off on holidays again? Hard hat. Denying you knew anything about a rape that took place 50 metres from your office. Definitely hard hat.

3. Make an announcement

One of the things I've realised over the years is that people are always asking you to DO things. Like putting out the bins or having a climate policy. But a little trick I learnt early on is that if you just say you'll do it, people will usually take you at your word. They'll often even print a glowing front-page feature piece about it.

It means you never actually have to do anything about climate change. And Jen will put out the bins.

4. Re-announce a previous announcement

Every couple of months or so it's worth rolling out an old announcement and making it sound like it's something entirely new.

This is especially effective if it involves spending money on some sort of program. I've promised $50 billion to the arts sector since I've been PM, simply by repeatedly re-announcing a $2,500 funding scheme from 2017. Do you want me to put the bins out Jen?

5. Blame the states

If people question why you haven't done anything about a certain issue, even though you've had over a year to plan for it, be sure to label it an issue for the states.

This works even if the issue is stipulated in the nation's constitution as being a Federal responsibility.

6. Set up an enquiry

Enquiries give the impression of vigorous activity, when in fact it's just some overpaid ex Liberal Party member printing out a templated findings report before heading off to the Tattersalls Club for a cigar.

Make sure your enquiry lasts for as long as possible – enough time for everyone to forget what the enquiry was about in the first place - so they can instead concentrate on the new photo you've released of yourself eating strawberries on the back of an army tanker. Wearing a hard hat.

A SHORT, SHARP 7 MINUTE DINNER THAT WILL ACTUALLY LAST 6 MONTHS

THE NORTH FACE

Uber Eats

Indentured labour never tasted so good!

Christian Porter Ordered To Pay $550,000 To Jo Dyer, In Humiliating Backdown By Jo Dyer

Former Attorney General and supposed legal expert Christian Porter has been ordered by the Federal Court to pay theatre and film producer Jo Dyer more than half a million dollars, in what Porter described as a humiliating backdown by Ms Dyer.

A smiling Mr Porter said he felt vindicated by the decision. "It's pretty clear who the winner is out of all of this," he told journalists outside the court. "And that's the guy standing in front of you with a half-million bill to pay off.

"I know whose shoes I'd rather be in right now, and it certainly isn't those of the person who's about to have all of their legal costs paid by me".

Mr Porter said this proved he had come out of the case untarnished. "The judge couldn't be any clearer. I am to pay $550,000 in costs, Ms Dyer is to receive $550,000 in costs. How absolutely embarrassing for her".

Scott Morrison Says He Is Willing To Accept Responsibility For Brisbane's Successful Olympics

Admitting that he regrets not confronting the issue earlier, a repentant Scott Morrison says he is now willing to accept that he, and he alone, is responsible for Brisbane's successful bid for the 2032 Olympic Games.

"This one's on me. Not the bid committee, not the Queensland Premier. I have to own this," the Prime Minister said in what appeared to be a rare admission.

"When you're in the top job, there comes a time when you have to put your hand up and say, 'I was responsible for that incredible win that will bring international investment and attention to Australia and totally reshape the nation's third largest city. I need to be accountable for the positive media attention that results from an international victory like this'.

"That's the long and short of it. The fact is, this is a historic day, not just for Brisbane and Queensland, but the entire country. And I have to take responsibility for that".

10,000 New Cases Of Fuckwit Confirmed In Melbourne

Protesters Believe Government That Can't Even Organise A Vax Rollout Is 'Controlling Them'

Thousands of protesters in Sydney and Melbourne believe that a government that misplaced $60 billion last year, had to bribe voters to secure the election and can't even manage to organise a vaccine rollout with 18 months' notice is controlling their every move.

"They're tracking you right now," one protester said of the Government that last year spent $20 million on a COVID app that has failed to track a single case.

Others were even more wary of trusting elected officials. "You break one of their so-called laws and they will chase you down. They know exactly what you do and where you live," one woman claimed, apparently unaware of the fact that this Government is so useless at tracking people it had to serve just about every single Centrelink recipient with a Robodebt notice because it couldn't identify the tiny percentage of people who actually broke the rules.

Another man said Scott Morrison was listening in on his phone calls. "I know for a fact he's listening in on my calls," he said of the man who wasn't even motivated enough to call the CEO of Pfizer.

The man said he had posted his concerns on Facebook, Twitter, YouTube and Reddit. "People need to know that they're being tracked".

Greg Hunt Starts Cutting Pfizer Vax With Phenylacetone, Baking Soda To Stretch Out Stash

Lockdown Announced In Byron Bay, Healing Crystals Already Sold Out

Tamworth Locked Down To Prevent The Spread Of Barnaby

Morrison Reminds Olympic Athletes That It's Not A Race

Labor Holds Emergency Meeting To Discuss How To Fuck Up Their Lead In The Polls

Senior Labor MPs and party strategists joined a hastily-organised call this morning, after the latest Newspoll revealed there was significant work to be done to orchestrate a disappointing loss at the next election.

With Labor a full eight percentage points ahead of the Coalition, many within the party worry that the path to a come-from-in-front-defeat is becoming more difficult to envisage. "There's a lot of ground to make up. It's getting harder to see how we can pull this off," one insider said.

Opposition Leader Anthony Albanese urged calm and asked his team to draw on previous experience. "This is a big gap, but there's no need for panic. We've fucked this up from here before, and we'll fuck it up again. Trust the process, trust the plan".

While the date of the next election is still unknown, Mr Albanese said there was still time to snatch a last-minute defeat. "We have time on our side. If we're disciplined enough to match the Coalition on every single policy, eventually voters will see that there's no point voting for us. Let's not give up now".

Many Labor MPs who spoke to The Shovel on background said there was a sense of growing unease within the party, particularly amongst backbenchers. One said his future was on the line. "I'm in a marginal seat, so when I look at these polls, there's a growing realisation that I may need to spend the next three years working in Canberra. It's looking pretty grim".

THE SHOVEL NEWS IN BRIEF

AUGUST

Christine Holgate To Receive $1 Million From Australia Post, Will Be Left In Safe Place If No-One Home

Police to replace rubber bullets with pop-up vaccination clinics to help disperse anti-vaxxer protesters more quickly

Fragments Of Integrity Found In Canberra Wastewater

Canberra residents are on high alert this evening after authorities detected what appeared to be traces of honesty and decency in wastewater samples. Experts quickly dismissed the news, saying the sample – which would be the first positive trace in the capital in more than 350 days – is assumed to be a false positive.

"We're pretty sure this is a mistake in sampling, or an historic case of integrity shedding," a spokesperson for the Water Authority said.

She urged Canberra residents not to be concerned, confirming it is only a tiny trace. "We know this is not something we usually see in Canberra, so it may make some people uncomfortable. But we're confident that, even if this does turn out to be a positive sample, it will not spread easily to others".

The levels of bullshit detected were at normal high levels.

Kmart Plate 'Embarrassed And Remorseful' After Being Videoed In Same Room As Nadia Bartel

A Kmart plate that featured in a viral video has released a statement this evening, saying it is "embarrassed and remorseful" for being videoed in the same room as Nadia Bartel.

In a short post, the plate asked for forgiveness and said it hoped to re-earn the public's trust.

"I have let you all down by my actions. I am incredibly embarrassed and remorseful for my conduct. It does not reflect the flatware's brand or values", the plate stated.

"For many years, my colleagues and I – the hard-working cups and bowls of Kmart – have prided ourselves on our association with people who are famous for reasons other than being the ex-partner of an ex-football player. We can, and will, do better.

"I take full responsibility and I am committed to taking all necessary steps to ensure I make better choices in future".

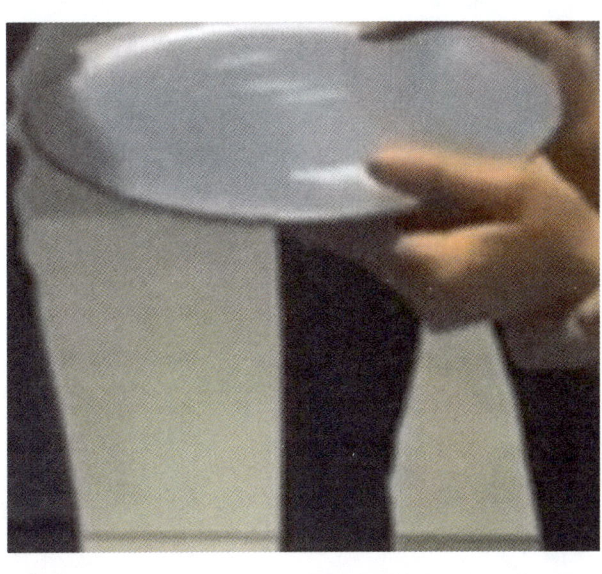

Pro-Lockdown Rally Held In Sydney

A pro-lockdown rally in Sydney has been hailed a huge success after absolutely no-one turned up.

Millions of people across the city did not come to the rally, which didn't begin in the CBD before not spreading to suburbs across Sydney.

One participant who wasn't at the rally said the protest stretched further than the eye could see. "Not a single person for kilometres. Incredible".

Police, who didn't attend the rally, said there were no arrests. A man didn't punch a horse.

'Question Everything' Says Man Who Believes Absolutely Anything

A man who believes the coronavirus is a hoax that is transmitted via 5G phone towers controlled by Bill Gates through a secret paedophile network funded by Hillary Clinton, says you sheeple will believe anything that is fed to you.

"Wake up! You're being fed lies!" said the man who refuses to get vaccinated because he watched a YouTube video once that said vaccinations contain secret microchips that are used by Hollywood actors to control the world for Satan, evidenced by the fact that the word 'Pfizer' is actually code for 666 when you change the letters into numbers and turn a few of them upside down".

Urging his friends on Facebook to 'question everything', the man shared a link he had just been sent, but not fully read yet, that provided unequivocal proof that 9/11 was faked by a secret government agency funded by George Soros.

"Don't just blindly accept what people tell you," the man said, adding that he had been waiting all day by his computer for Q's next update on 8chan about how to free the enslaved minds of the world.

COVID-19 virus says it will charge a $273 accommodation allowance for each night it has to stay in Canberra

Biden Comforts Terrified Defence Contractors: "There'll Be Another War Soon"

President Joe Biden has provided reassurance to the nation's traumatised defence contractors, promising that America will enter another pointless, unwinnable 20 year-war before they know it.

"There, there, buddy" he said as he leaned in to embrace a CEO of one of America's largest arms manufacturers. "I know it feels confronting, frightening, terrifying right now. I feel you. But this period of uncertainty will pass. We'll be there for our military industry, as we've always been in times of great need. We'll get you out of this".

One tearful defence industry executive said he appreciated the President's kind words, after what had been a distressing two weeks. "What we've witnessed in Afghanistan these last few weeks has been difficult for everyone to watch. Horrifying stories of military orders not being renewed; shocking pictures of scaled-back defence contracts; terrified sales executives who may never meet their targets for the 2021/22 financial year. This is nothing short of an emergency," he said.

Biden said he heard their concerns. "Know that you can trust your government to find an obscure country that most Americans cannot even locate on a map, to engage in a meaningless two-decades-long war. We will not abandon you".

Melbourne protest demands

Pull up nappies with Spiderman on them
Daytime nap to end immediately
Tiny Teddy biscuits (the ones with chocolate)
Sticker set
Spade for sandpit
2 hours of cartoons every morning
Big boy bike
Cuddle from Mum
Royal commission into vegetables
Royal commission into mandatory bedtime
Mass distribution of Coco Pops and icecream

US payments giant Square has purchased Afterpay for $39 billion, which it will make in four easy payments of $9.75 billion

Hillsong Completes Transformation Into Mainstream Religion, After Leader Charged With Concealing Sex Crimes

After years of being cast aside as a fringe movement, Hillsong Church can finally be considered a conventional, mainstream religion, after its founder Brian Houston was charged with allegedly concealing information about child sexual abuse.

Mr Houston said Hillsong had been fighting for acceptance within the broader Church system for years.

"Even having a Prime Minister as our supporter didn't garner us the respect of one of the big boys. We were increasingly worried we'd become a joke, or be forced to blackmail weird lonely celebrities, like Scientology does. We just weren't ready to do that just yet.

"Sure, we're technically Christian, and we follow all of the core principles of Christianity, like not paying taxes. But still, people weren't treating us like a real religion.

"Then it occurred to us - we need dark secrets. All of the top religions carry some version of a dark shame. Most involving children".

Reverse Parallel Parking Confirmed For 2024 Olympics

Parking a car parallel to the road in line with other parked vehicles while others look on and judge will be an Olympic sport in Paris 2024, it has been confirmed.

The International Olympic Committee (IOC) said the addition of the popular spectator sport was long overdue.

"Running 100 metres in under 10 seconds is difficult, but not nearly as hard as driving a car backwards into a small space with the radio blaring, while someone in the back seat tells you they could do it better," a spokesperson said.

The event will include a number of different rounds, including 'parking between two SUVs', 'parking with an opinionated passenger' and the gold medal round 'parking right out the front of a pub while 100 people look on'.

Unlike other Olympic events, judges will make loud comments and unwelcome suggestions from the passenger seat while the competitors are in action.

To increase the difficulty level and to mirror real-life competitions, participants will be asked to drive in a car that is clearly too big for them.

Inspiring! Olympian Competes Without Backstory

In a stunning example of overcoming adversity, an Australian swimmer has contested an Olympic freestyle heat without a single inspirational story about the obstacles she had to overcome to realise her dream of competing at the Games.

The only competitor to enter the pool without a backstory, Sam Smith didn't let the setback deter her, finishing fourth in what will surely be remembered as one of the stories of the Games.

Smith said it was always her dream to compete in the Olympics and that she wasn't going to let the lack of a backstory stop her. "It's been an amazing journey. To get here, against all odds. It's an amazing feeling.

"You see all the other swimmers out there with moving backstories, about overcoming adversity, and you wonder how you can compete. It can be a bit intimidating; there were moments when I thought I didn't deserve to be swimming at this level. So it's a special feeling. It just proves that even people without a backstory can overcome hurdles and make it at the highest level," she said.

First Time Ever That Something That Started In Sydney Has Taken Off In Melbourne

A niche movement that began life in Bondi is starting to go big in Melbourne, marking the very first time anything that's originated in Sydney has actually taken hold in the Victorian capital.

"Usually we wait to see what Melbourne's doing, give them shit about it and then copy it six months later," Sydney trend observer Mia Worthington said. "But this time it's the other way around. They haven't even got their own variant!"

She said she struggled to think of anything that's started life in Sydney going big in Melbourne. "Colonisation I guess? Gelato Messina maybe? But that's not exactly going viral is it. Pretty sure they haven't got a Gelato Messina in Bacchus Marsh."

Toddler Ready To Be Interviewed On Commercial Radio After Not Shitting His Pants Today

Labor Narrowly Avoids Developing Policy

Morrison Says Afghanistan War Was Responsibility Of The States

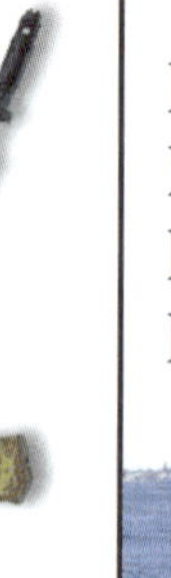

PM Unveils Major $90 Billion Distraction

"My Family Is More Important Than Your Family" Morrison Says In Emotional Address To Nation

A tearful Scott Morrison has provided an explanation for his cross-border Father's Day trip to Sydney at the weekend, saying he loves his family more than you love yours.

Acknowledging that hundreds of thousands of Australians were unable to see their families on Father's Day – even if they lived in the same city – the PM said that it was because they don't deserve to.

"I sat down with Jen and the kids on the weekend and we chatted about this. We said, why is it that I can ignore border closures during a pandemic while the rest of NSW, ACT and Victoria can't? How am I able to get my weekends away paid for by the taxpayer? And the thing we came back to, again and again, is that I'm special and you're inconsequential," Mr Morrison said, his voice cracking with emotion.

"I get up here day in day out and I say that all Australians are equal; that if you have a go you get a go; that we're all in this together. But the truth is, you're meaningless. I only ever think about myself".

Stopping to take a sip of water as his eyes welled up, the PM said Father's Day was really important to him.

"The thing about Father's Day is it's all about me. It's not about Jen. It's not about the kids. It's about me. And that's what I love about it. That's why it's so important to me. I think I deserve that, don't you?

"And yes, many people have told me that they would've liked to have seen their family on Father's Day too. And to them I say, I'm sorry that you're so irrelevant. But I'm not going to spend time thinking about other people, I'm not, because, because ... sorry, this is quite emotional for me ... because the truth is, I've got enough on my plate thinking about myself".

ICAC Concedes It Should Have Checked With Berejiklian First To Find Most Suitable Time To Investigate Her Corruption

Anti Vaxxer Shocked To Discover He Carries 'Driving Passport'

A Port Macquarie man who says a vaccine passport is a contravention of the 1948 United Nations Universal Declaration of Human Rights, was astonished this morning to discover a 'driving passport' had been sitting in his wallet since 1996.

"I never signed up for this," said Richard Mallison, 42, who took his driving test at the age of 17 and renewed his licence four years ago. Pulling the offending card from his wallet, a shocked Mr Mallison called friends to ask if they had seen anything like it before. "It's got your photo on it, your address, your name. Everything! And I've had this thing on my person every day for over two decades".

Putting on his seatbelt and reversing out of his driveway, Mallison let out a panicked squeal as it dawned on him that the passport was legally required in order to access certain activities. "Next thing you know you'll need one of these things to get into a pub".

Gladys Daily Presser Cancelled After Poorly Received First Season

The much-anticipated NSW reboot of the popular VIC Daily COVID Presser has been cancelled after a poorly received first season. The last episode will air on Sunday.

With scores of 30% on Rotten Tomatoes and an audience rating of just 8%, the cancellation came as no surprise to critics, who said the cast was 'unrelatable', 'callous' and 'incompetent, but not in a fun The Office kind of way'.

"I never found it believable," one critic wrote. "In one early episode the main character laughs that she doesn't believe in lockdowns, and then the rest of the season she spends berating people for not following the rules of lockdown. I'm all for suspending disbelief to a point, but this was a bit over the top".

Another critic said the show was becoming too predictable. "Pretty early on viewers worked out that if the central character said she definitely wasn't going to do something, she'd end up doing that exact thing six episodes later. It was a fun twist the first time, but they became easier and easier to pick".

Another said it was boring and tiresome. "Poor writing, repetitive scripts, longwinded monologues. I stopped watching after the first few episodes. Zero stars".

The abrupt cancellation means the show will end at an odd point in its narrative, with the action rising to a crescendo, rather than being resolved.

Sister show VIC Daily COVID Presser has been renewed for another 48 seasons.

Scott Morrison says he is concerned about whether Christian Porter's blind trust has breached Ministerial Standards and will seek further advice from Christian Porter.

Union Claims Protesters Weren't Real Tradies: "There's No Way They'd All Turn Up On Time"

The CFMEU has blamed outsiders for yesterday's violent rally, saying the idea that two hundred tradies would all turn up at the specified time was fanciful.

In a strongly-worded statement, the union said the punctuality of the protesters was a tell-tale sign they weren't members.

"This was clearly a group of well-organised extremists. The protest had a 12 noon start time yesterday. Our members are aiming to be there between 6am and 4pm today, but more likely Thursday or Friday. They'll call when they're on their way," the statement read.

The union also said that the style of the protest made it clear tradies weren't involved. "When our members attend a rally, generally one will protest while five or six others stand around in a circle and look on. That didn't happen at this rally".

Gladys To Avoid ICAC By Joining Federal Politics

In an emotional speech today, Ms Berejiklian said it was time to take a step back from the constant scrutiny of state politics and do something less demanding. "After four and a half years in the top job, I need to give myself a rest. I need a break from the expectations, the daily press conferences, the scrutiny and the anti-corruption hearings. In short, I need to spend some time on the Liberal Party front bench in Canberra".

She said being held accountable to the electorate day-in-day-out took its toll. "It's gruelling. As a member of the Morrison government, that's one less thing I'll have to worry about. Perhaps I could become Health Minister or Attorney General – something where you don't need to be answerable to the people for every little thing. Or every big thing".

Maryland GovPics / Wikipedia

After our print deadline

Child Surprised To Learn Santa Dresses Up As Dad For Other 364 Days A Year

Pauline Hanson Condemns Term 'Black Friday', Saying 'All Fridays Matter'

Unclear If Star Wars Present For 42 Year-Old Man Or 4 Year-Old Son

Trick-Or-Treater To Dress Up As 'Marginal Liberal Electorate' In Order To Get Bigger Handouts

Eight-year-old Ryan Saxon will walk his local streets dressed as Liberal electorate on a margin of less than 3% this Halloween, in a plan that he believes will secure him significantly more loot.

Tossing up whether to go as 'Chisholm', 'Wentworth' or 'Boothby', the grade three student said he hopes to net at least $500,000 for his efforts.

"It seems to be the way things work around here – I'm not sure why nobody else has thought of it to be honest. Going dressed up as a vampire or a skeleton is great. But it's not going to net you the cash you need to upgrade your lawn bowls club is it?" the boy said.

He said his strategy was pretty simple. "My plan is to just go up to each house and say 'I need half a mil to upgrade the women's change rooms at my country club, hand over the cash or I'll put you out of Government'. I reckon the money should flow pretty quickly".

Saxon's elder sister, who is going dressed as a real-estate agent specialising in parcels of land close to airports, is confident of securing $30 million.

THE SHOVEL
NEWS IN BRIEF

BREAKING
Scott Morrison Wishes Australians A Merry Christmas "From Me, Jen And The Whole Image Management Team"

Look at the top right of the page

Columns

'Whoops! I Forgot To Buy Enough

By Greg Hunt

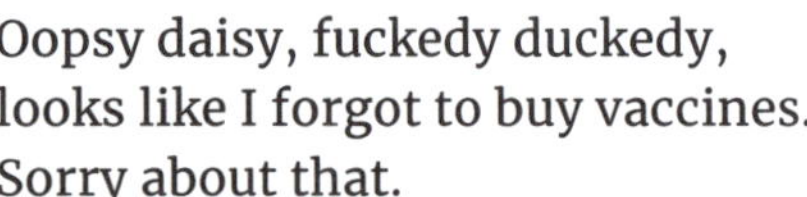

Oopsy daisy, fuckedy duckedy, looks like I forgot to buy vaccines. Sorry about that.

It means we're a wincey bit short, and I can sense some of you are a little bit angry with all the kerfuffle. But with the utmost respect, can I just say – how was I supposed to know that we'd need enough vaccinations to cover the entire population?

Easy to say now when we're watching everyone else overseas get vaccinated. But not so obvious in June last year when we were in the grip of the deadliest pandemic in a century. Twenty-twenty hindsight and all. And to be fair to me, I had more important things to worry about back then, like undermining a lockdown in Victoria.

Look, the truth is, I did intend to get more. But then I saw this great offer for a cheaper vaccine, and I thought, well if you're going to scrimp on something, this is the thing to do it on.

I saved us $2 billion dollars by not taking up those offers from Pfizer and Moderna. Sure, we conservatively lose that much money every week when a major city has to shut down. But how are those two things even remotely related?

So, yes, it's a little bit of a hassle now, but let's not overstate it. Australians can be reassured by the fact that we'll have everything running tickety-boo at an unspecified time in the future.

Anyway, gotta fly. I'm off to the pub with a dozen colleagues and I promised them I'd buy a round of three cheap beers that none of them wants.

Australia Day: "No-One Can Tell Me To Stop Celebrating The Anniversary Of Captain Cook's 334 Not Out Against The Advancing Japanese Troops At Gallipoli"

By Robbo Johnson, The Shire, Sydney

There's been a fair bit of talk about moving the date of Australia Day recently. But these people don't have any idea what they're messing with. 26th January is sacred. Mark my words, it 'aint moving.

Do all the complaining you want. But buggered if you'll stop me celebrating Cooko's triple century against a full-strength Japanese attack on a deteriorating Gallipoli wicket in '44-'45.

It was the making of this country. Bob Hawke gave the nation a day off to celebrate. And yet here we are, trying to mess with it.

For those Australians, or should I say unAustralians, who don't like it, it's time for some truth bombs. Gallipoli is one of the toughest grounds to play in the world. They don't call it 'The Kokoda Track' for nothing.

A three-month journey on a tall sailing ship to get there. Uncovered wickets in those days as well. And despite everything that was thrown at him, our captain - Captain Cook – stood firm. Stood up, in fact, and said 'No! We won't pay our gold mining licence fee just because you tell us to'.

It was a turning point. An uprising. It forged the character of this nation. As Ned Kelly famously said about the game at the time, "I come from the land down under".

But of course these whingers wouldn't know that because they don't study history. Don't know the significance of that day. Don't understand the blood that was spilled. And they never will because they don't want to listen.

Shame.

7 Reasons Why The Desk's Claim That It Was Masturbated On Should Be Questioned

A liberal staffer is accused of performing a sex act on a female MP's desk, and within hours he's lost his job. That's how the rabid media works these days. Cheering on the downfall of an innocent man until they get their way. This is the mob at work, where proof doesn't matter and facts that don't suit get played down or suppressed.

But let's stop for a moment to consider what really happened on the night in question. Was the desk really defiled by this man? Maybe. But maybe not. Let's be brave enough to ask some probing questions about this sordid affair.

What was the desk doing in the MP's office in the first place? Don't you think it's strange that a desk would be in Parliament House, alone late at night? What was it doing there? Did it have security clearance? Or was there an ulterior motive?

Why didn't the desk report this at the time of the incident? It's very convenient that this is released to the media now. Just as the government is getting on top of its other sex scandals. If this really happened, why wasn't it reported to police at the time?

Was the desk drunk? We're not supposed to ask this question, according to PC culture. But these things matter. Had the desk been drinking? And if so, how much?

Even if this act did occur, how do we know the desk didn't consent? This is the problem with these issues. It's he said/desk said. Maybe the desk wanted to be ejaculated over. If we'd had a proper process – like a consent app – we'd know.

Is this just a simple case of regret? The desk wakes up the next morning, regrets what it's done and now takes it out on this poor man, ruining his career in the process. We've seen it a hundred times before.

Why didn't the desk just leave the MP's office? It's got functioning legs. If it didn't like it, why didn't it leave? Isn't it more likely that it wanted to be there all along? And was the desk even Australian anyway?

Why was the desk out alone? I'm sorry, but desks need to take responsibility sometimes. Why was it out alone at night in a place as dangerous as Parliament House?

THE SHOVEL NEWS IN BRIEF

August

Army General To Draw On Iraq, Afghanistan Experience – Expects To Have Vaccine Rollout Complete In 19 Years

Editorial

Surely there's a more efficient way for Craig Kelly to find a sexual partner than randomly texting 12 million Australians

By The Editor

No doubt about it, lockdowns are hard. A lot of Australians are struggling. A lot of Australians are lonely. But a lot of Australians aren't sending unsolicited text messages to half the population.

It's a pretty inefficient way to find a sexual partner, Craig. Use Tinder, mate. Grindr if that's more your thing. Join a seniors meet-up group with your local council – pretty sure they'd be doing online events at the moment. But ease up on the texts. It's just a little weird mate. It's scattergun.

One of the great things about the dating websites is that you can get matched to someone who shares your interests, rather than just going for a blanket approach. So for example, you might put in your profile something like, "Lazy, taxpayer-funded conspiracy theorist seeking likeminded knobhead to read 4chan hydroxychloroquine forums with" and you'll be away. Before you know it you'll be popping horse wormers and screaming 'I love Q' with the woman of your dreams.

It's a better way to go about it mate. You know it makes sense.

THE SHOVEL NEWS IN BRIEF

BREAKING

Craig Kelly Denies He's An Anti-Vaxxer: "It's The Microchips I'm Worried About"

Boring Stuff

Direct your lawsuits at

Editor
Caz Smith

Editor-at-Large
Charles Firth

Copy Editor
Veronicah Larkin

Subscriptions
subscriptions@chaser.com.au
Phone: 02 8227 6486
Fax: 02 8227 6410
Address: PO Box 161
Hornsby NSW 2077

2021 Contributors

Correspondents
Asha Leau
Anthony Bell
John Delmenico
Tom Basso

The Interns
Aleksa Vulovic
Gabbi Bolt
Harry Sekulich
Lachlan Hodson
Zander Czerwaniw

Contributors
Alex Apollonov
Amy DarbyShire
Anthony Bell
Anthony Jucha
Brenton Fuessel
Bridget Fox
Craig Reucassel
Daniel Patrick
Dave Piepers
David Lopis
David M. Green
Dom Knight
Gideon Rozner
Hamilton J. Tyler
Harry Sekulich
Isaac Stewflay
Ivan
Jackson Harding
Jeremy Langridge
Jess Wheeler
Joel Pragnell
Julien Furnace
Kathryn Mcleod
Matt Hudson
Matthew Davis
Phil Brandel
Phil Jeffrey
Rohan Arneil
Sam Asher
Sam Pesaturo
Sam Voller
Simon Fraser
Solomon Frank
The Honi Soit Editors 2021

And to anyone we've accidentally forgotten, rest assured you were only left out because we hate you.

The Chaser Quarterly

The Chaser's Disclaimer Managing editor: Charles Firth. This is the twenty first issue of *The Chaser Quarterly*, and is published by Chaser Digital Pty Ltd (ACN 141758812) of 330 Wattle Street, Ultimo. While effort has been made to verify any facts contained within this publication, no responsibility will be taken for errors or omissions contained herein by Chaser Digital Pty Ltd, its officers, employees or their agents. Readers should rely on their own enquiries when making decisions touching on their interests. Apart from satirical articles which discuss public figures for the purposes of humour, any mention of any person, alive or dead, is entirely coincidental. We expect readers to use their own common sense in determining the truth or otherwise of any statement in this publication. *The Chaser Quarterly* is available in newsagents and bookshops across Australia, and is printed by Spotpress, 24-26 Lilian Fowler Pl, Marrickville, NSW, 2204. Subscribe at **chasershop.com** and stay up to date at **chaser.com.au**

Oh, you again

WHAT A GREAT YEAR! If you overlook the pandemic, mouse plague, lockdowns, earthquake, riots, and return of *Hey Hey It's Saturday*, then I think we can all agree that 2021 was the best year in memory. And if not climate change will soon see to that.

As for the Chaser, as always we have gone from strength to strength. Whether it was inadvertently becoming the only news site in the country when Facebook banned all our competitors, blackmailing two former Prime Ministers into giving us $100, or that time we found a free burger in the bin outside our office that was only half eaten, it's been a nonstop string of successes for The Chaser if you don't listen to those pesky accountants.

Sure we hit a few small bumps when various politicians threatened us with lawsuits for saying things like how [redacted] likes to [redacted] with [redacted], but much like Christian Porter, we forced them all into humiliating backdowns by simply rolling over and paying them a lot of money. Checkmate.

And while normally we wouldn't praise a year where the Prime Minister almost caused a war with France over a submarine deal and threatened to shoot all women, where Barnaby Joyce somehow ended up getting re-promoted to Deputy PM, and where the words 'parliamentary wank desk' entered common parlance, at least we can say this year there isn't an out of control American President telling everyone that vaccines are a hoax. We now have Craig Kelly for that.

In any case, congratulations for surviving another year, or if you didn't then we're slightly worried about how you're reading this. We hope you enjoy the next 66 pages of typos as much as we enjoyed creating them.

Happy reading,

The Chaser Interns

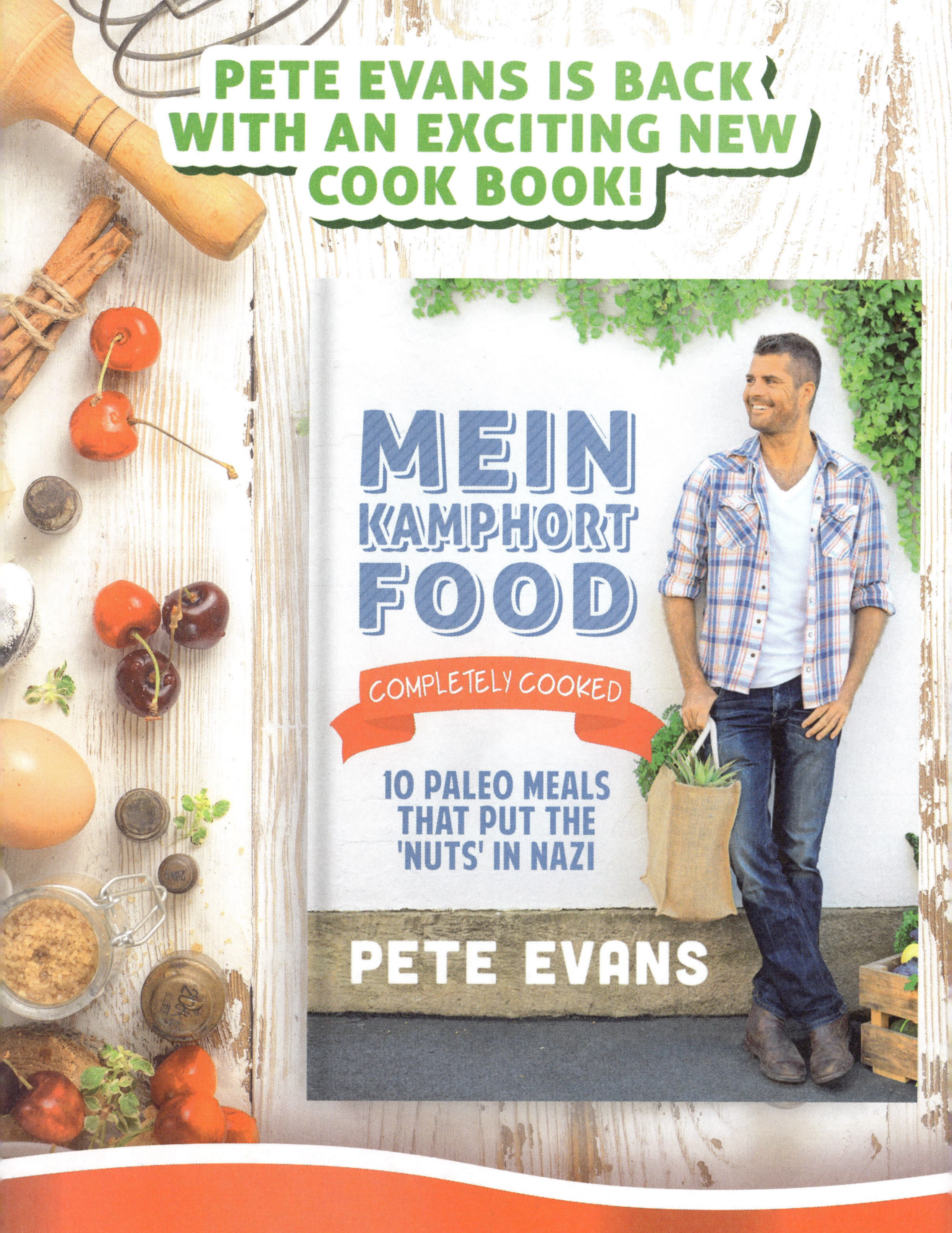

The reich recipe for every occasion

Real headlines that could be The Chaser

The news is barely distinguishable from satire these days, and to prove it, here's a selection of 2021's most unbelievable headlines that sound like they should have been one of ours.

Scott Morrison says politicians will no longer be exempt from laws against sexual harassment

Chinese safari park 'sincerely sorry' for not telling public about escaped leopard

'Everyone makes mistakes', says teen who karate-kicked 74-year-old man into River Mersey

Iowa man who stole election sign goes on to steal newspapers that reported it

Lawmaker says he owes hammers apology after calling opponent 'dumb as a bag of hammers'

Petition urging Jeff Bezos to buy and eat the Mona Lisa gains steam

Minister claims car park program 'very transparent' after refusing to release documents

Trump White House threatens to fire anyone who tries to quit

DOORDASH SPENT $5.5 MILLION TO ADVERTISE THEIR $1 MILLION CHARITY DONATION

A Parkland shooting survivor's dad found QAnon and is now convinced the massacre was a hoax and his son was a paid actor

A drunk man who had been reported missing spent hours with a search party looking for himself, report says

People Can't Vacuum Or Use Their Doorbell Because Amazon's Cloud Servers Are Down

Trump warns if Biden's elected, "he'll listen to the scientists"

Anti-gay Hungarian politician József Szájer resigns after breaching Covid rules to attend 25-man orgy

Mom Calls 911 Because She Didn't Like Son's Haircut

Tim Cook says employees who leak memos do not belong at Apple, according to leaked memo

A Profanity Filter Banned The Word 'Bone' At A Paleontology Conference

BBC sets up complaints line for 'too much TV coverage' of Prince Philip's death

OnlyFans to ban sexually explicit content

Boris Johnson considered being injected with COVID-19 on TV to prove it isn't dangerous

Authorities beg Americans not to kiss chickens amid Salmonella outbreak

French workers can now eat lunch at their desks without breaking the law

JANUARY

Breaking: America

Trump forced to ride out twitter ban by reorganising his top friends on MySpace

Trump: "I did not lose my Twitter access, I won it by a landslide"

AMERICA FORCED TO TOPPLE OWN GOVERNMENT AFTER RUNNING OUT OF FOREIGN ONES TO OVERTHROW

Keen watchers of "The United States of America" have praised the "refreshing" new direction of the show, after the latest episode featured a surprise twist where America invades itself for a change.

However some viewers have expressed dismay at what they are describing as "lazy and unbelievable" storytelling, claiming the whole last season of *America* was a complete mess.

"It's gone completely off the rails!" complained one viewer online. "Do you seriously expect us to believe that there's a riot in the middle of a plague, and meanwhile the President is trying to overthrow an election and everyone just goes along with it? Jesus this makes Game Of Thrones's last season look well written by comparison."

The once popular series has suffered a series of setbacks in recent years, with writers struggling to compete with rival program The United Kingdom for viewership. "Ever since the Trump plot twist, the two shows have gone out of their way to out-drama each other," explained TV expert Miles Tulong. "Boris Johnson the messy haired populist leader was clearly just cribbed straight from the United States's plotline, and the US had to go even further. Next thing you know Trump has COVID, he's banning twitter, and drinking bleach."

"The whole thing's just ludicrous now, do they seriously expect us to believe a bunch of ragtag idiots could storm the Capitol of a country that spends a trillion dollars on the military every year? Give me a break."

Socialist revolutionary Biden begins the slaughter of billionaires

Fruit picking shortage solved by Michael McCormack's massive effort cherry-picking facts

Trump takes election to 'highest court' in a special episode of Judge Judy

PUTIN RESIGNS AFTER LOSING AMERICAN ELECTION

Russian President and famed Dobby the house elf impersonator Vladimir Putin has today stepped down from his role as the leader of Russia, after losing the American election.

"Da, it is very disappointing," Putin is reported to have told advisors. "Maybe I will shoot down a civilian passenger plane, that always cheers me up."

Putin will be best remembered for his legacy of killing any journalists who write bad thing about him, and also having a really tiny penis and horribly bad br

TRUMP DROWNS HIS SORROWS WITH A STRONG GLASS OF BLEACH

Internet troll and part time President Donald J Trump has today sat down to survey his legacy over a nice chilled glass of '18 vintage Clorox.

"Well my business empire may be in ruins, I may owe hundreds of millions in taxes, my reputation and name might be mud, and I may have been indirectly responsible for the deaths of 400,000 people," smiled Trump, "but at least I built my wall. Well, part of my wall. Also it was a fence. And Mexico didn't pay for it. But I got to keep this White House pen so I think we can chalk the experience up to a win."

The President, who lost all houses of government in just one term, only months after contracting a deadly virus, and weeks before causing an angry mob to storm the capitol, sighed wistfully as he thought about all the lives he managed to improve during his term as President. "Just think of Little Jimmy the billionaire stock trader who can finally afford to buy his family a third yacht with his tax breaks. Or my lawyer Michael Cohen who... oh damn I forgot Michael's still in jail, completely forgot to pardon him. Oh well, I guess you win some you lose some."

Morrison's approval rate drops to 2% after suggesting Australians could use Bing if Google blocks Australia

AUSTRALIA DAY RENAMED "RUBY PRINCESS DAY" IN COMMEMORATION OF ANOTHER BOAT THAT FUCKED EVERYTHING UP

The Australia Day argument has been settled once and for all today, after the Federal Government announced a compromise designed to make nobody happy, ensuring true balance is reached across the political spectrum.

"Today I'm proud to announce we're not changing the date, but also we're no longer celebrating the founding of Australia," announced Scott Morrison. "Instead we will now be using January 26th to commemorate a different boat arriving and fucking everything up – happy Ruby Princess Day everyone!"

The news comes as Scott Morrison attempted to put out multiple fires from recent incorrect comments surrounding the basic facts of Australian history, including a claim that Australia never had slavery, and that Morrison knows how to use the bathrooms at McDonalds. "Clearly the historical record suggests that Morrison is wrong in this case," said Sydney University Historian John Beard. "Just ask anyone who has a descendant that worked at Engadine Maccas and the oral history is irrefutable."

Ruby Princess Day will be celebrated with a public holiday, in which all Australians will be required to stay home and avoid friends, family and any kind of fun, because a few entitled fuckwits decided to spend their downtime on a giant floating fossil fuel pump attached to a gastro petri dish.

"Brilliant, now I feel terrible, but it's in a way that Rupert Murdoch's papers can't deny the cause of," said one local man. "Oh wait no I forgot NSW has a Liberal government. Deny away Rupert."

Confused Pauline Hanson joins Invasion Day protests against 'foreigners coming and taking over'

GOVERNMENT THAT WON'T SHUT UP ABOUT BOAT PEOPLE CAN'T UNDERSTAND WHY INDIGENOUS PEOPLE ARE UPSET

Immigration Minister and part time monster mash Peter Dutton has today joined the chorus of voices calling for Australia Day to be scrapped, after learning the day celebrates the time a group of criminals travelled by boat from overseas to invade a sovereign nation's borders.

"This goes against everything I stand for," wept Dutton. "All this time I thought I was celebrating the genocide of brown people, when in actual fact I was supporting something I find morally reprehensible. I am disgusted."

Asked what he thought about other similar holidays, such as ANZAC Day, where Australians join together to celebrate invading Turkey by boat, Dutton said he felt faint, and needed to sit down. "All my life has been a lie," whispered Dutton. "What's next, is someone going to tell me that MY family came here by boat?"

Dutton was then rushed to hospital, after being informed that Boxing Day involves a giant boat race, Christmas celebrates a man who travels the world without a passport, and the Queen's Birthday celebrates a foreigner who lives off government benefits.

Witnesses did not have the heart to tell him about Labour Day.

NURSE COMING OFF A DOUBLE-SHIFT DEVASTATED TO HEAR A MODEL HAD TO WASH HER OWN HAIR

The world was hit with devastating news this week, after reality star turned model Vanessa Sierra lived through the tragic experience of washing her own hair while stuck in the hotel quarantine. The noble and brave sacrifice was reportedly made so her partner Bernard Tomic could play in a world famous tournament of a sport he admits to not liking and only does for the millions of dollars he wins.

In response, a late stage protest is being organised by a nurse who just found out about the crisis after missing the news due to her having to work a double shift.

"We all have had to make sacrifices but obviously this has hit some people harder than others," she explained. "I mean, I can't even imagine what it would be like to be in a position where you have to choose between cheering on your multi-millionaire boyfriend or having your hair professionally washed twice a week."

Although not everyone has been as inspired by the tragic tale of a rich influencer going two weeks without a blow dry, some in the media have even mocked the poor victim.

"Wow imagine being so rich and spoiled," said one breakfast TV host. "It was like I was telling my driver, stylist, and the hair and makeup ladies, this influencer is so disconnected from the rest of the world she needs to have everything done for her. It's absolutely disgusting."

"Now we'll just take a quick break so I can have my makeup touched up."

"We must act now" Morrison horrified to learn climate change will affect footy season

Man insists support for lockdown is unrelated to forgetting to buy Valentines Day gift

Family finally get government to fund childcare by changing kid's name to "Coal"

MAN WHO SPENT $200K ON EMPATHY CONSULTANT UNABLE TO WORK OUT RAPE IS WRONG

Prime Minister of Sydney Scott Morrison has today expressed his heartfelt condolences to a staffer who was sexually assaulted in Parliament House, after being informed by his wife that this kind of thing is really not on.

"After a lengthy consultation with my wife and kids I have decided I am not pro-rape," said the man who has clearly wasted the $200,000 he spent on empathy consultants. "I know a lot of you out there in the community will struggle with me taking such a controversial stance on this issue, but Jenny has insisted that it's important I look at this issue as if it affected me personally, which gave me a whole new perspective on the topic."

This is just the latest in a long string of decisions by the Prime Minister that have been guided by his wife's unusual access to a thing called 'emotions'. "Why only yesterday I was walking down the street" explained Morrison. "and I was going to punch a small child in the face, but then Jenny said to me 'think about how you'd feel if that was one of your kids' and I immediately changed my mind. She's a real philosopher my Jenny."

LABOR IMMEDIATELY SCRAPS PLAN FOR SCOMO STYLE NAME FOR ANTHONY ALBANESE

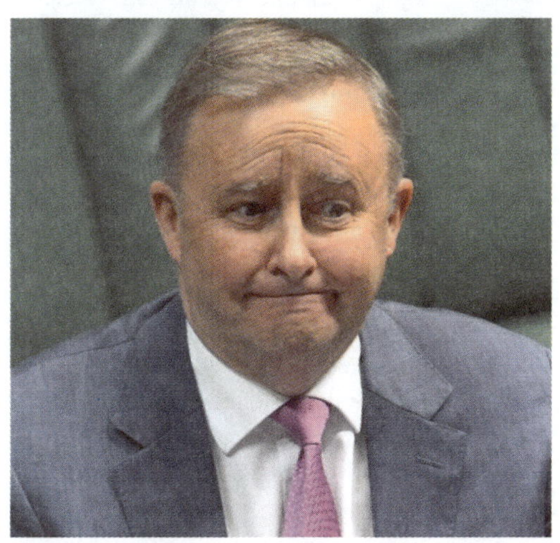

Labor strategists have today floated, and immediately scrapped, plans to introduce a catchy new nickname for Anthony Albanese in the style of Scott Morrison's 'ScoMo', after the team decided to just move right on with the meeting after a moment of reflection.

"Yea uh, I think we'll table that to circle back on at a later date," said one senior Labor figure while aiming a rifle at his own foot, "let's just move right along to point two – Penny's opening speech to the National Union of Students, so now if you can all open the document titled P-NUS we'll get right to work."

The move comes as the Labor Party struggles to find ways to make the beer drinking, DJing socialist seem fun and relatable to the common man. "I think it's time we pulled out the big guns," said one Labor party strategist. "We announce some great policies that benefit the working class, unify the factions to show we're ready to govern, and then right at the last minute we'll knife him for a less popular leader. They'll never see it coming."

Fire-fighter sets kitchen on fire after being told to work from home

YOUNG COUPLE BUYS HOUSE WITH NOTHING BUT HARD WORK, DETERMINATION, AND $2.5 MILLION LOAN FROM PARENTS

THE CHASER NEWS IN BRIEF

January
"Vaccines aren't safe" claims friend who used to say you could go home if the teacher was 5 minutes late

'TEACHERS INAPPROPRIATELY GAVE KIDS CLIMATE LESSONS' COMPLAINS GUY WHO INAPPROPRIATELY GAVE STUDENT LOVE LETTERS

Former teacher Alan Jones has voiced his concerns to Sky News viewers that school teachers are 'inappropriately' teaching kids about issues such as climate change, potentially distracting from the most important parts of education like being given love letters by your teacher.

"How are students supposed to have a steamy secret affair with faculty members if they're all stressed out about the end of the world?" asked Jones. "Someone needs to step up and teach these students, and since no one else will I guess I will, if I have to."

In response to Alan's criticisms, the teachers who can still pass a working with children check have stated they couldn't be more relieved. "This is great news. It would be a real cause for concern if that guy was telling us that everything we do with students was appropriate. You can tell you are doing something right when Alan Jones complains about you."

Sydney scraps lockout laws, leaving only Sydney's venues, citizens as reason not to go out

FACEBOOK FINALLY CRACKS DOWN ON RACISM BY BANNING ALL AUSSIE MEDIA

Facebook CEO and Wallace and Gromit character Mark Zuckerberg has today hit back at suggestions that he isn't doing enough to combat the tide of racism, sexism and conspiracy theories on his site, after pointing out he just banned the Sky News facebook page.

"We just dealt with a whole heap of white-supremacist groups," said Zuckerberg, "whether its the Daily Telegraph whipping up stories about Muslims turning kids into vegan wind turbines, Alan Jones casually dropping an N-bomb on air, or simply breakfast TV holding a lighthearted panel on whether the holocaust was really that bad, I think we can say we're all better off without this cesspool in our lives."

"Even the few non-racist news outlets couldn't seem to stop platforming people like Steve Bannon and Milo Yiannopoulos. One minute the media gets mad at us for 'not banning them sooner', they the next minute invite these people on to their shows! So we've decided to just cut off the problem at the source."

REPORT: UH OH

Editors at The Chaser have said "aw golly, shucks, what a pickle" today after Mark Zuckerberg declared that the news content ban on the Facebook platform would extend to satire sites, despite them not qualifying for Google's billion dollar news payout.

Asked about the ban, and whether not being hamstrung by Facebook would mean news organisations are finally free to say what they think about him, Mark Zuckerberg said he finds goats really attractive. "Does anyone else find them really sexy, or is that just me?" said Zuckerberg, before smearing himself in jelly. "Now if you'll excuse me I hear there's a boomer somewhere who has been radicalised by conspiracy theories and I must urgently do nothing about it."

12 **Daily Mail reader struggling to cope without crucial updates on Rebel Wilson's weightloss**

FACEBOOK RESTORES DAILY TELEGRAPH PAGE AFTER REALISING THEY'RE NOT REAL NEWS

The Facebook corporation has today apologised to News Corp after a mixup which saw sites like The Daily Telegraph and The Herald Sun banned as part of a wider removal of news content on the site. "We have now restored most News Corp mastheads to our platform," announced a representative this afternoon. "After careful analysis, we have concluded not a single one of their stories contains a shred of factual reporting."

The newspaper giant, which is best known for its stories claiming Melbourne is being over-run by invisible African gangs, convinced Facebook of their lack of qualification as a newspaper after showing them a single column by Andrew Bolt. "Oh sorry we didn't realise you were a fiction publisher," said Facebook after reading a Bolt article on how the bushfires were a ploy by big science to destroy the coal industry. "Also I never realised that coronavirus is a hoax. Well you learn something new every day."

The platform has also moved to restore beloved chef and neo-nazi Pete Evans to their platform, after his instagram page was inadvertently caught up in the ban. "Sorry we only ban news content, not crackpot conspiracy theories," said the platform. "We now return you to your usual feed of racist uncles and people who claim Hillary Clinton is selling children from a pizza shop."

CHANNEL 9 JOURNO FORCED TO HIT STREETS TO INFORM PUBLIC ABOUT GREAT SAVINGS AT HARVEY NORMAN

Local TV journalist Brad Ligma has today risked his life by stepping out of his air conditioned inner-city studio in order to interact with the public for the first time in his career. "Yea it's a bit unusual," admitted Brad, who would normally simply spend the day copying and pasting news stories from the ABC, "but the public must be informed about how great K-Mart's summer sales are."

However a deflated Brad returned hours later without having convinced a single member of the public of the importance of the new vacuum cleaner BOGOF sale. "It's as if they don't even care," said a stunned Brad. "Don't these people know this is crucial news. Not like that garbage about the Ebola outbreak in Africa. Gosh, imagine being the kind of sellout hack who does that kind of reporting. How could you sleep at night?"

"Not as well as you'd sleep if you pick up one of the great bargains being offered by Mr Snooze this April, that's for sure."

Anti-Vax Facebook mum glad to see her 'real news' sources are still available on Facebook

"WE DON'T MANIPULATE THE NEWS" SAY EIGHT MURDOCH MASTHEADS IN UNISON

News Corporation CEO and world's largest prune Rupert Murdoch has this week shown his complete lack of influence over the news in Australia, after eight national mastheads all ran variation on the same anti-Rudd hitpiece, in what many are describing as an amazing coincidence. "Wow, what are the odds," asked one surprised reader. "All these newspaper editors from completely different states all decided to hold the same editorial line on this and every other topic. It's weird how this keeps happening isn't it?"

However, News Corp has hit back at the idea that these front pages confirm the organisation has an agenda, with all 8 editors flatly denying any such suggestion in unison, after checking with Rupert first to make sure that's okay.

"Australians are smart people who make up their own minds about what media they consume," said one of the corporation's soleless husks. "Which is why we have to rely on government handouts and money extorted from big tech companies to keep our mastheads in print."

"It's important that we have a diversity of views in the media, and News Corp provides an essential part of that diversity," explained another executive. "We all know how important it is for a healthy democracy to have the largest news distributor in your country owned by the resident of another country who has no problem spreading dangerous lies if it will help his share portfolio. Whatever would the national debate do without this crucial voice?"

Rupert Murdoch was not available for comment on this piece due to a prior commitment to steal candy from children.

HARRY AND MEGHAN ANNOUNCE COMPLETION OF THEIR ONE MILLIONTH INTERVIEW ABOUT HOW THEY JUST WANT THEIR PRIVACY

In a series of touching exclusive interviews, The Duke and Duchess of Sussex have tearfully spoken to Oprah Winfrey, James Corden, Stephen Colbert, Jimmy Fallon, Jimmy Kimmel, Conan O'Brien, Trevor Noah, David Letterman, Samantha Bee, John Oliver, Chris Matthews, Wolf Blitzer, Anderson Cooper, Jerry Seinfeld, Howard Stern, Zack Galifianakis, Marc Maron, Joe Rogan, Ira Glass, Michael Barbaro, Jon Stewart, Barbara Walters, a BuzzFeed intern, Kyle and Jackie O, random Redditors, the host of Holey Moley, some guy Meghan met in Whole Foods who just started a podcast, Johnny Carson via seance, and even Ellen DeGeneres about how desperate they are to stay out of the public eye.

They did, however, turn down an appearance on The Project, stating they're not THAT desperate.

 Royal Family says sorry to Meghan Markle by offering free driving-tour of Paris

EXPERTS ADVISE AGAINST TAX BREAKS FOR THE RICH OVER FEARS THEY WOULD JUST SPEND THE MONEY ON DRUGS

THE CHASER NEWS IN BRIEF

February
Shock as company that lets drunk addicts pour money into machines rigged to lose is found to be unethical

MEDIOCRE COUPLE NOT CHEATING ON EACH OTHER DESPITE BEST EFFORTS

Local couple Greg and Michelle Baxter have today renewed their commitment to each other, after completely failing to find someone better despite their best efforts. The couple, who have both been working late and taking Latin dance classes for months now, has so far failed to introduce a single homewrecker into their loveless marriage, with even the strange hippy couple across the hall not yet having probed whether they're in an open marriage, despite months of fondue nights.

"You're the only woman for me," said Greg putting his arm around Michelle as he envisaged what life could be like with one of those supermodels from Instagram. "And I'm not just saying that because my secret Tinder isn't getting any hits."

Michelle has also expressed her undying tolerance of Greg, at least until the dust finally settles from Brad-from-Accounting's divorce.

"We're in this for the long haul babe," Michelle said, presumably referring to the fact that every minute she has to spend listening to Greg monologue about Wes Anderson feels like a lifetime. "It's just you and me, until the moment my pottery instructor stops ignoring my innuendos."

Facebook news ban over, Daily Telegraph returns to rightful place as nation's top comedy site

MARCH

Morrison denies Liberal Party sexism problem - "Just ask our old Minister For Women"

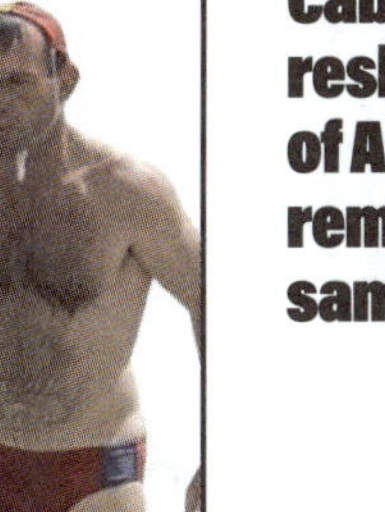

Cabinet reshuffled, ruler of Australia remains the same

Michaelia Cash announced as over acting Attorney General

PM MEEKLY ASKS COLLEAGUES IF THEY CAN MAYBE EASE UP ON ALL THE RAPING FOR A BIT

Scott Morrison has today taken swift and decisive action on the scandals engulfing his government, by kindly asking his colleagues if they could maybe look into trying to not rape quite so much in future.

Speaking at a packed meeting of Coalition ministers, backbenchers, and staffers, the Prime Minister was firm but understanding. "Look, I'm not trying to tell you all what to do, I'm not one of those mean bosses that forces everyone to wear suits and turn up at 8 sharp, but you know all this constant sexual assault is starting to become a bit of a distraction," explained the PM. "I'd much rather the public focus on the great things we're doing for the country right now, like helping our mates rort JobKeeper and making life more miserable for welfare recipients."

"It would be really swell if you all could perhaps put a bit more effort into easing up on the whole sexual assault thing until after the election."

Morrison has also announced a series of internal reforms in response to the furore. "I want to assure the Australian people that we're taking action on these rape claims," explained Morrison, "and you can rest assured we will all be trying much harder in the future to make sure nobody finds about this stuff."

JOURNALIST PUTS FINISHING TOUCHES ON A CHRISTIAN PORTER STORY THEY PREPARED LAST NIGHT FOR NO REASON...

Pictured: No one in particular

Local journalists have allegedly woken up this morning to put some finishing touches on a story that they wrote about Attorney-General and [redacted] Christian Porter last night that will allegedly be released some time today, for 'no particular reason'. None whatsoever.

"You always want to be prepared with a story like this," said the journalist who definitely wants to stay anonymous after getting off their phone with their lawyer. "It's a story that is about nothing. I don't know what you're talking about. Just a normal story about a boring mundane announcement that I am not waiting for him to make today. Can a journalist not just write a casual story about the Cabinet Minister whose Wikipedia has just been updated with information putting him in Sydney in 1988? Allegedly."

FACE MASKS ARE NOW COMPULSORY IN THE REACTOR CORE

Dear Staff,

I think I mentioned a few weeks ago that there's a small leak here at the Chaser Springs Nuclear Reactor and Childcare Centre. If you didn't get that email you might want to check your spam filter, it's fairly important, especially the bit about taking iodine tablets.

At the time, I assured everyone that there was nothing to worry about and it would sort itself out. Turns out, these things don't sort themselves out. Who knew?

Now I know many of you have been begging me to make it compulsory to wear masks in the affected corridors, especially where you can literally see the clouds of gas wafting out from the reactor core.

But I didn't want to jump too fast onto that bandwagon. You see, I believe in a little thing called freedom. I know that some of you (especially the shouty ones) think not getting radiation poisoning is a priority, but what about the people who don't care about radiation poisoning? I have to run this facility on behalf of everyone, not just the safety nuts who would have this facility shut down every time people start dropping dead.

Anyway, I've listened to what my safety officer was telling me eight weeks ago, and I am now making masks compulsory in all corridors where you can visibly see wafts of green smoke (unless you are going for a jog through the green smoke, in which case don't worry about it.)

And the great news is that now that face masks are compulsory, the need to fix the leak is basically redundant. Instead, I'm proposing that we learn to live with this deadly radiation leak (or in some cases, die). It'll be much easier than fixing it.

Unfortunately, there aren't enough face masks for the children in the Child Care Centre part of the building, but I'm sure they'll be fine. As long as 80% of adults wear face masks, then things should be able to get back to pretty much normal.

Charles Firth
CEO
Chaser Springs Nuclear Reactor and Child Care Centre

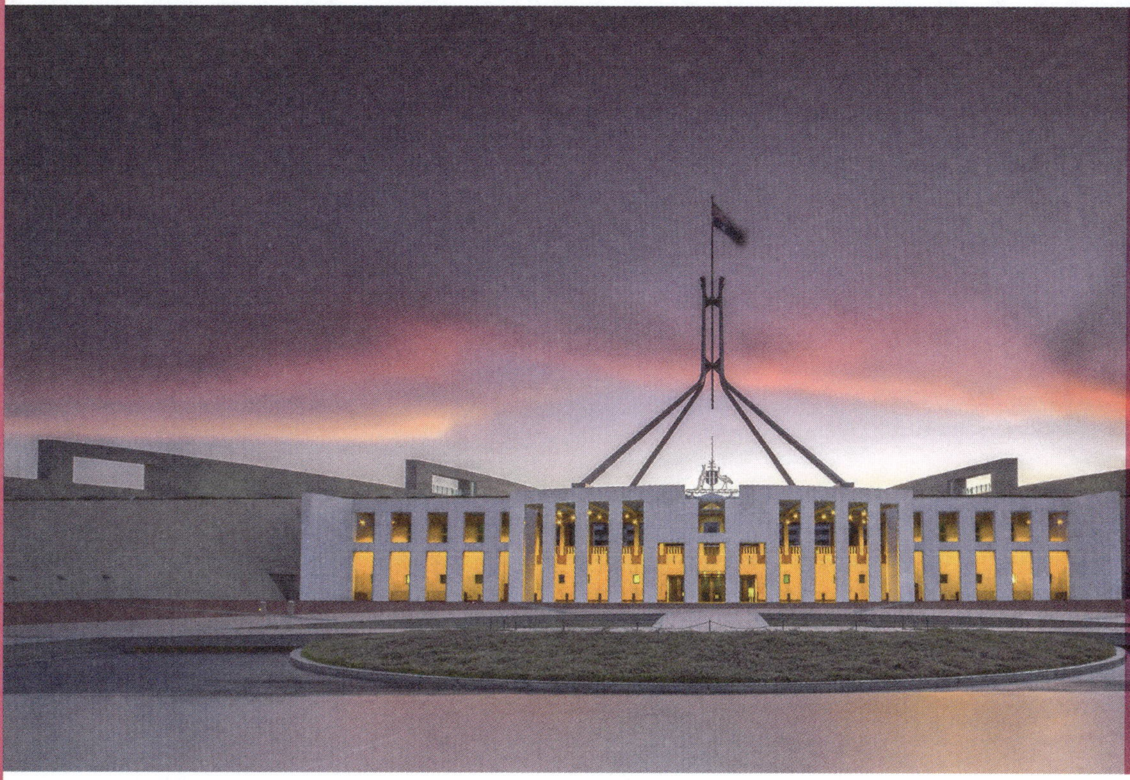

Life Hack: How not to rape someone in one easy fucking step

Rape is a thing you obviously shouldn't do, but for many politicians "ethics" doesn't always come naturally. Luckily this really, really simple life hack can help you avoid some awkward situations during your next term in office:

Step 1: Don't fucking do it, just don't rape!

For this step, if you are going to engage in a sexual act with another person all you need to do is simply make sure you have enthusiastic consent and if you don't have it, do nothing. Literally do nothing at all. Don't make the active choice to rape them. You will find it is easier and better for everyone if you don't do it. If you need to ask in order to double check if you have consent, it is definitely really fucking worth it. And that's it, that's all the steps.

Way too frequently asked questions:

But isn't consent a confusing concept?

No, no it really really isn't. If you are only doing sexual acts based on 'implications', if they gave consent then told you to stop during, if they are too young, if they are too drunk, if they said no but you continued pursuing until they 'gave in', if you asserted a level of power you have over them, if they aren't conscious, or literally any other situation where they are not in a right state of mind and are not enthusiastically consenting, you are in the wrong. It's pretty easy to understand, just assume you don't have consent unless you are directed otherwise.

Wouldn't asking for consent ruin the mood?

Not many people consider 'the person I was with wanted to make sure they weren't raping me' as a deal breaker, and if you are worried it will kill the mood for them chances are they probably weren't enthusiastically consenting in the first place. Unless of course you mean your mood, in which case you can always 'go fuck yourself' instead. Figuratively and literally.

If my friend or colleague rapes someone, should I help them hide it?

First of all, real concerning you are still using the term 'friend' when referring to them. But more importantly, NO! Fuck No! Holy Shit No! Have some decency you monster.

POLICE CALL OFF INVESTIGATION AFTER BURGLAR "CATEGORICALLY DENIES" ROBBING STORE

Police trained at the Morrison Institute for Crime Investigation have today solved every crime in Australia after asking the perpetrators if they did it, and then just letting them go if they say 'no'.

"Shockingly, it turns out that 100% of criminals in our murder investigations were wrongly accused," explained one officer. "Even the ones where there was overwhelming evidence turned out to be innocent. It's really changed our perspective on crime."

The new investigative technique, devised by Prime Minister Scott Morrison when investigating staff members, is expected to save law enforcement billions of dollars over the next ten years. "Finally we can allocate money to where it's really needed," explained one officer. "Like strip searching random teenagers on public transport. Because nothing makes people feel safer walking down the street than the threat that a bunch of adults might force teenagers to take their pants off. Round of applause for the boys in blue."

However, the police commissioner has since been forced to intervene in the situation, stating that releasing people just because they say they're innocent is unacceptable. "The fact is we've looked into this and we've discovered many of the people we were about to let go were actually black," explained the commissioner. "As a result we have launched a new round of investigations to ensure these people aren't at risk of committing further crimes, such as walking down the street while black, sleeping peacefully in bed while black, or walking their dog in a public park while black. These are the kinds of things we as police simply won't stand for. Unless they're a member of federal cabinet, in which case, carry on."

LIBERAL PARTY PRESS CONFERENCE FORCED TO RELOCATE AFTER REALISING THEY'RE WITHIN 500 METRES OF A SCHOOL

The Chaser Publishing Corporation has today been forced to shut down after spending thousands of dollars on lawyers' fees trying to craft this headline in a way that won't get them sued out of existence.

"Yeah, originally we had a very funny [redacted] about the [redacted]," said one writer tied up in the basement of the Chaser offices. "But then it turned out [redacted] had hired a defamation lawyer and we immediately [redacted] our pants."

Asked whether this headline has anything to do with the [redacted] [redacted] who [redacted] a 16 year old, members of the Chaser said that any such allegations are extremely defamatory and threatened to sue anyone who makes such unfounded claims.

"We've asked the writer whether this was a shallow attempt to sidestep defamation laws and they have 'strenuously denied' the claims," explained one Chaser editor. "As such, we're just going to presume he's innocent and not investigate any further."

"If anyone has a problem with this we'll be happy to escalate the matter, all the way to the attorney general."

Nation starting to suspect there might be a few reasons why Liberal Party is so resistant to an ICAC

AUSPOST TO DOUBLE EFFICIENCY BY SKIPPING 'PRETENDING TO DELIVER IT' STEP

Australia Post has today announced a new policy for its parcel delivery drivers, which will see their efficiency doubled by skipping the part where drivers pretend to do their job.

Officials say the change came after an audit of their processes suggested the charade of walking up to someone's door and then immediately leaving a note saying they weren't home was a complete waste of the drivers' time and led to unnecessary pollution, costs, and pissed-off customers all around the country, which was the only upside.

The new policy will see all parcels dropped straight to the post office where the recipient would be picking up, cutting out the ceremonial charade of driving the packages around as if they were going to actually try deliver it, despite everyone knowing that would never happen.

The government has responded to this announcement by reminding AusPost not to use the money for bonuses given out as watches, which the LNP has called "the largest waste of taxpayer money since we had to bin all those Back In Black mugs."

NATION SHOCKED THAT MAN DETAINING CHILDREN ON ISLAND PRISON ISN'T GREAT AT ETHICS

The nation of Australia has today expressed very convincing shock upon news that nobody in the Liberal Party seems to have any sense of workplace ethics. "Wow are you telling me a bunch of rich entitled private school kids who landed a cushy government job straight out of college are sexist and don't know what's appropriate at work?" asked the nation. "Colour me shocked."

The nation expressed equal amounts of shock at revelations today that Prime Minister, and man who once took off on a tropical holiday while the country was on fire, is also completely lacking in a sense of decency, after he tried to use conference about sexual assault to point score against a journalist. Morrison has since apologised for the incident, stating he is very sorry that Jenny would let this happen, and that he has now hired an empathy consultant to better help her understand why she was wrong to have not stopped Scott.

20 **Morrison announces cabinet reshuffle over fears staffer might have had sex on it**

GUY WHO STEPPED DOWN OVER ONE BOTTLE OF WINE FEELING PRETTY STUPID THESE DAYS

Former NSW Premier and last man in politics with a shred of integrity, Barry O'Farrell, has today decided he might still have a chance at a second crack at politics, after learning you can pretty much do anything these days and get away with it, if you just refuse to step down.

"Yeah, I must admit I felt my face go a bit red when I first heard Gladys had secretly been giving preferential treatment to her side piece without any blowback, but it was the middle of Covid," explained O'Farrell, "so I assumed that was an exception and I had still done the right thing. But now that a guy's been all over the media for a week having been accused of raping someone, and his temporary replacement is a woman who 75% of people were demanding resign over corruption less than two years ago, well I'm starting to think I probably didn't need to step down over being given a bottle of wine after all."

"I don't know when it was exactly," continued O'Farrell, "but somewhere between Angus Taylor being caught forging a document to smear an opponent, Dutton getting busted handing out visas to his mates' nannies, Greg Hunt liking porn on twitter, Barnaby Joyce rorting water holdings, Michaelia Cash getting busted tipping off the media about union raids, Bridget McKenzie pork barrelling sports grants, and the time Scott Morrison drove a large dump truck of cash up to News Corp headquarters and just poured the money into Rupert Murdoch's swimming pool, somewhere around this time I started to think maybe what I did wasn't so bad after all."

"Anyway, gotta go. I've got a cushy government job that was handed to me by my mates that I need to attend to."

NEW CABINETSAFE APP WILL TRACK IF YOU'VE BEEN IN CONTACT WITH AN ALLEGED RAPIST

Authorities have rushed out a new app to allow members of the public to keep track of whether they've come into contact with members of the Federal Cabinet.

Called CABINETSafe, the app is designed to allow users to track encounters with alleged rapists, people who support alleged rapists, people who cover-up for alleged rapists, people who don't read the reports about what alleged rapists have done, people who call a rape victim a "lying cow", and those think that continuing to be in Cabinet with any of these people is in any way acceptable.

"As a result, it covers everyone in the Cabinet," said the designer of the app.

Symptoms of being a cabinet member include a loss of moral compass, blurred vision for what Australia should be like in 2021 and delusions that they can escape the consequences of their actions.

Authorities say that members of the public should take precautions if they do come into contact with a member of the Federal Cabinet. "If you do happen to be in the same room as them, leave immediately and for God's sake, make sure you sanitise your hands."

The spokesperson said that ideally we wouldn't need an app like this "but it appears that nobody in power seems to be doing anything about it. They seem to think that the problem will just magically go away without doing anything."

The app maker says that future updates will include the ability to track contact with corrupt members of Cabinet. "We didn't put that in the first edition because there's just too much data to deal with on that."

LINDA REYNOLDS OFFERS APOLOGY: "I'M TRULY SORRY EVERYONE FOUND OUT WHAT I SAID"

Defence Minister Linda Reynolds has today made a heartfelt apology for referring to Brittany Higgins as a "lying cow", expressing deep regret that this fact was made public.

Reynolds, who is presently taking mental health leave due to the severe stress of being held accountable for her actions, issued the following statement: "You know, obviously hindsight is 20/20, but were I able to do things all over again, I would definitely have made sure nobody found out what I said about that nasty [expletive removed]. I wish to apologise unreservedly to Scott Morrison and the Government for my failure to conduct a better cover-up. Christ, I can't believe the mess that [expletive removed] has put us in. Oh, crap, did I say that out loud?"

According to the Chaser's sources, Reynolds' colleagues haven't been totally placated by the apology, seeing her inability to sweep this under the rug and shift the blame to Labor as a serious breach of traditional Liberal Party values. The Prime Minister is backing the embattled minister however, telling reporters: "Look, I was going to throw the book at her, but then Jenny reminded me how I would feel if my own daughters had been caught insulting a staffer who had been raped by another of their staffers in their ministerial office, so now I've changed my mind, and instead I'll build her a chicken coop."

SUNRISE REASSURES FANS THE LOSS OF ARMYTAGE WON'T STOP THE SHOW'S CONSTANT RACISM

Sunrise viewers were shocked this morning at the announcement that Samantha Armytage will be standing down from her role as host in order to spend more time making racist gaffes. Producers for the popular breakfast show have announced that they are deeply saddened to be losing one of the shows largest liabilities but they have reassured fans that the loss of Armytage won't stop the show's constant racism.

"It's going to be tough to replace her," said a Channel 7 executive after asking the show's defamation lawyers to stop cheering so loudly, "she had such a unique voice. Many journalists want to fight for marginalised groups with arguments based on facts, but not Sam. From her mocking a UN representative who wanted to talk about the refugee crisis, her calling for a second stolen generation, to when she literally cheered on a girl for being white; Sam brought something to the show that we previously tried to keep more subtle."

Industry experts have been going crazy with the rumours of who could be the upcoming replacement, with names including Pauline Hanson, Lauren Southern, Katie Hopkins, Alan Jones, David Duke and many, many, oh so many other people in Australian media.

Morrison explains he was only vaccinated in case of emergency holiday to Hawaii

ENTREPRENEURIAL SYDNEY COUPLE DOUBLE HOUSE VALUE BY DOING FUCK ALL TO IT AND JUST WAITING 4 YEARS

Local Sydney couple James and Jane Watson have today been praised for their entrepreneurial spirit by realestate.com.au after they had the genius idea to buy a house with their parent's money, and then double its value by just waiting for four years.

"Yeah, it took a lot of hard work and dedication to just sit around doing nothing for four years, but it really paid off," said James. "That extra $500,000 me and the missus are now worth will really help us purchase three more investment properties using leveraged equity, and by pushing other millennials off the property ladder we'll be able to easily pay off those extra mortgages through our eye-watering rental prices we'll charge while doing absolutely no upkeep on the property and gaining millions more in property value. It's a perfect system."

Asked whether this might actually be a waking hell for anyone under the age of 40 who wasn't lucky enough to buy into property before the bubble, the government Minister for Housing said that was a very good question, before giving homeowners another tax break and putting a bid in for 12 more houses.

GERMAN IMMIGRANT FAMILY CONCERNED WHETHER THEIR GREAT-GRANDSON IS ENGLISH ENOUGH

A family of German and Greek immigrants to the UK has expressed alarm that their great grandson is not English enough, according to an interview with the child's mother and father.

Though the specific Windsor family member who expressed concern was not named, everyone knows it was Prince Philip.

"It is outrageous that Harry would marry someone who wasn't from England," said Prince Philip, who was born in Greece, to Greek and Danish heritage. "I can't stand the idea that a foreigner would marry into our family. It's mixing up the bloodlines."

The Greek-born Prince married into the Windsors. Until 1917 the Windsors were known as the Saxe-Coburg-Gotha family, thanks to their German heritage.

The royals have strenuously denied that the concerns raised were in any way racist, in much the same way that Christian Porter has strenuously denied all accusations against him.

A MESSAGE FROM THE MINISTER FOR THE ENVIRONMENT

The IPCC isn't the whole story, it's just 3900 pages of it

Dear Constituents,

I know some of you are alarmed that the IPCC report on climate change released this year says that the planet is on track to being an unliveable hellish inferno by about next Tuesday.

However, as the Minister for Climate Change I've skimmed the 3900 page document and there are several flaws in their methodology that makes me think perhaps things are not as gloomy as the report makes out.

First off, nowhere was it noted in the report that plastic straws are being phased out around the world. In fact, by 2025, the planet will be largely plastic-straw free. And yet this was not factored into any of the calculations made by so-called 'scientists'.

This is despite my government's $50 million advertising campaign against plastic straws in the lead up to the last election.

Same goes for single-use plastic bags and plastic cutlery. By 2035, our takeaway cutlery industry will be dominated by wooden sporks. (Sure, the sporks may lead to a few more trees being cut down, but you get the general drift). In fact, Australia will be a global leader in wooden sporks by 2100. In fact, we'll have a net-zero amount of plastic cutlery by 2167 (if you don't include knives or spoons).

Not only that, but the IPCC completely fails to take into account the little "Eco" button that is now included in most major brands of air conditioner, and in many SUVs. This is an example of the market leading the way in carbon abatement, and shows that the government is right to wash its hands of all responsibility for it.

But worst of all, I am appalled by the oversight of the IPCC to not include a single mention of Earth Hour in the whole of its report. How can we trust their calculations if they're not factoring in the crucial role that turning off some light bulbs in some houses for an hour each year will have on the planet's carbon footprint.

What a joke!

Angus Taylor

Minister for Climate Change

PETER DUTTON SEEN IN NORTHERN NSW FRANTICALLY TRYING TO STOP THE BOATS

Home Affairs minister and McCains mascot Peter Dutton has today pledged to stop the growing tide of boat people seeking asylum from NSW, by threatening to deport them to Nauru.

"I'm sorry but if you're facing trouble in your homeland and want a better life, you're going to have to look somewhere else other than Australia," Dutton told fleeing crowds today. "You can't be coming down to southern NSW and taking people's jobs while there are still open places in India and Pakistan's asylum program."

Instead the navy has been instructed to tow all boats to Papua New Guinea, where they will be kept in indefinite detention for millions of dollars a year.

"This is the only choice," said Dutton visibly twitching with ecstasy. "I'm afraid there is simply no other option than to put more children in detention. Oh dear sorry I appear to have salivated on the microphone."

NSW FLOOD SOLVED AFTER ANGUS TAYLOR SELLS OFF ALL THE WATER

Minister for Emissions Reductions and guy you have to watch your wallet around, Angus Taylor, has today taken drastic action on the floods engulfing NSW, by immediately selling all the water to a mysterious shack located on the Cayman Islands.

"It's a great day for NSW," said Angus, handing a mysterious suitcase to Barnaby Joyce. "Now if anyone needs me I'll be retiring to my new super yacht, which I bought with money I ... inherited. Yes that sounds like something they'd believe. What do you mean my microphone is still on?"

The super yacht was impounded shortly after by Peter Dutton after hearing a boat was off the coast of Australia

'We need more women in the Liberal Party, but not if that means fewer men' says PM

APRIL

Morrison deploys emergency Jenny to explain racism to the royals

"Same-sex marriage is immoral" says organisation covering up decades of child abuse

PM realises he somehow missed the crucial 'starting the vaccine rollout' step of the rollout

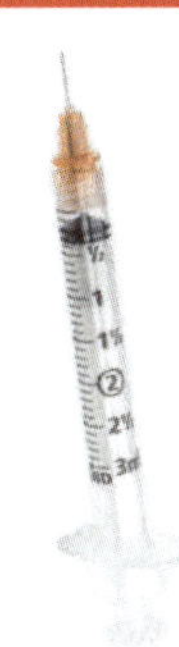

"MEGHAN FAR TOO ENTITLED TO BE A LITERAL PRINCESS" CLAIMS TABLOID

MAN WHO LOOKS LIKE A POTATO SUES PUBLIC FOR MAKING FUN OF HIM

Free speech campaigner and man who is suing someone over a mean tweet, Peter Dutton, has today accidentally been turned into chips after being mistaken for a potato by a local chef. "God this potato is awfully bitter," said one customer biting into the chips. "Which, for the record, I would not make fun of if not for the fact that it also has a terrible personality."

However, a spokesperson for potatoes has today spoken out against the comparison to Peter Dutton, pointing out that at least potatoes aren't locking kids up on an island or white-anting their colleagues. "It's very cruel to compare this brainless vegetable to a potato," said the representative. "I'll have you know that potatoes have fed thousands of starving children, while Dutton simply keeps them in his basement."

When contacted for comment, Dutton's secretary said that he was not available for comment on this piece, as he only rises at dusk to terrorise local villages.

SCIENTISTS DISCOVER RARE DOUBLE-CENTAUR WITH BOTH HEAD AND BODY OF A HORSE

Sky News successfully debunks evolution by turning audience into Neanderthals

27 APRIL

RECORD ULURU RAINFALL: PAULINE HANSON UNVEILS PLANS FOR A NEW WATER PARK

After unprecedented rainfall drenched Uluru over the weekend, One Nation Senator Pauline Hanson has today proposed turning the sacred indigenous landmark into a water park to attract more tourist. "I have already lined up the finest lifeguards that Cronulla Beach has to offer" she said at a press conference on Tuesday. Amusement park experts have raised concerns that the abrasiveness of the rock-surface coupled with the length of the proposed water-slide would result in patrons being effectively skinned by the time they reach the bottom.

"We don't see skin colour anyway" the One Nation Senator responded, asserting that "Uluru belongs to all Australians, except those it belongs to, who shouldn't have a say in this."

SCOMO'S EMPATHY COACH WINS PEACE PRIZE AFTER STOPPING A MASSACRE

There has been big news out of Canberra today, as the $190,000 empathy coach hired to teach Scott Morrison to give a damn about other people has received a peace award after he heroically stopped the massacre of over 100,000 peaceful protesters.

"It was hard work but I am glad it all paid off," said the true blue hero today. "I'm just glad no-one was shot dead for being a woman. Anyone with empathy would do the same really – which has me very worried about what Peter Dutton might be up to."

"Now all we have to work on is the fields of 'fire victims need help', 'old people should be kept in liveable conditions', 'refugees are human beings', 'women are people too', 'unemployed people deserve to not starve to death', 'poor people aren't automatically criminals', 'black people shouldn't be murdered by cops' and 'rape is bad'. Other than those, Scotty's doing really well."

Scott Morrison sets aside April 31st to meet Brittany Higgins

27

MORRISON CLARIFIES REASON HE DIDN'T SHOOT CROWD IS HE'S TOO BUSY AIMING AT OWN FOOT

Prime Minister until Dutton gets the numbers, Scott Morrison, has today clarified his earlier comments stating that he should be praised for not shooting protesters, after revealing that the only reason he held back was he had used up all the bullets shooting himself in the foot.

"I think you'll find sometimes journalists are bad people too. Checkmate media," said Morrison today while carefully aiming a gun sight at his big toe and squeezing down on the trigger. "So maybe don't throw stones in glass hou… OW GOD DAMMIT IT WENT OFF AGAIN. WHY DOES THIS KEEP HAPPENING?"

This is just the latest in five separate incidents this week that has seen the Prime Minister and his staff shoot themselves in the foot in what doctors are calling the worst public health epidemic since Barnaby Joyce's sex life made headlines in 2018. "It's terrifying," warned one doctor, "what with every second minister taking health leave right around the time they get in trouble, the Liberal Party's finally living out their dream of completely crippling the public health service."

AUSTRALIA EXITS AFGHANISTAN AFTER LIBERATING COUNTRY FROM BRUTAL AUSTRALIAN FORCES

The children of Afghanistan have today breathed a sigh of relief, as Prime Minister Scott Morrison announced the withdrawal of Australian troops from the country.

The announcement, which came hours after President Biden's withdrawal of US Troops, marks the end of foreign occupation of Afghanistan by western combat forces. "Freedom is always worth it," Mr Morrison said. "Australians have always believed that and Afghanistan would not be free of Australians without our help."

The withdrawal comes almost ten years after the assassination of terrorist leader Osama Bin Laden and the death of 31,000 civilians. Newly-appointed Defence Minister Peter Dutton is reportedly shattered that he was not able to contribute to either figure.

"This isn't the time to discuss war crimes" says Prime Minister holding press conference about Afghanistan war

MORRISON REWARDS HIMSELF WITH NEW TROPHY TO CELEBRATE VACCINE ROLLOUT

Prime Minister Clott Morrison has today decided to reward himself for all his effort taking credit for the vaccine rollout, by buying himself yet another engraved office trophy to commemorate the milestone of having 3% of the country fully vaxxed.

Having successfully rolled the vaccine out to himself, Jen and the girls, his entire cabinet, and all marginal electorates, Morrison told journalists that this was a triumphant delivery of the vaccine to all the important parts of Australia.

When asked how it feels about Scott's obsession with covering it in commemorative trophies, Scott Morrison's desk replied, "Are you kidding? Do you have any idea how many worse things a parliamentarian's desk could be covered in?"

SCOTT MORRISON CLAIMS AUSTRALIA'S VACCINE ROLLOUT IS "A LOCAL COUNCIL RESPONSIBILITY"

Prime Minister for Men Scott Morrison has today slammed Australia's local councils for not having their constituents vaccinated. Stating that heads will roll for this monumental stuffup, the Prime Minister urged Australia's various local councils and community watch groups to "pull their fingers out" and get on with the vaccine rollout.

"As Prime Minister of the country, I am simply flat out dealing with the big issues such as sorting out bin nights and making sure the dog poo in the park is getting picked up. I can't be expected to deal with the national health programme as well!"

Asked whether he is sure that he is holding his "responsibility of each level of government" chart up the right way, Mr Morrison looked down at his notes and responded: "... shit."

The Office of the Prime Minister of Australia released another statement late last night confirming to those in the Norwood Payneham & St Peter's council area that next Tuesday it is yellow bin nigh, not green.

MAY

Gone too soon: Prince Philip dead at 182

Jeff Bezos files for divorce after learning marriage is a union

Banned from Facebook, Craig Kelly forced to turn to OnlyFans to spread conspiracies

PETER DUTTON VISIBLY ORGASMS AFTER HEARING ALL BOATS HAVE BEEN STOPPED

Minister for The Dark Arts Peter Dutton has today excused himself from a press conference after being asked how he planned to deal with the fact that all boats around the world have ground to a stop, at which point Dutton was seen to visibly twitch with ecstasy.

"Oh god, yes, oh yes, no don't stop," Dutton told the gathered journalists. "Now say it again but hold up a picture of some children in detention. I'm almost there."

A frantic Scott Morrison was then seen rushing to the scene to ensure Dutton didn't get any parliamentary desks involved.

Scott Morrison reassures the nation that he has received his vaccine

Tesla cars start killing their own drivers in bold next step towards fully driverless cars

DUKE OF EDINBURGH ASKED WHETHER HE WISHES TO MAKE ANY FINAL RACIST REMARKS

In unpromising news for the Royal Family, HRH Prince Philip, Duke of Edinburgh, has been asked by doctors tonight if he wishes to make any final racist remarks. The 99-year-old has been in hospital since last week, and it is believed his condition has deteriorated to the point where he is unable to even objectify his nurse.

"This is just a precaution at this stage," said a palace physician. "But we think it is prudent for his Royal Highness to make any bigoted, disparaging or prejudiced comments soon, just in case."

"He may even say something unpleasant about the Belgians, the Brazilians or the Nepalese," they suggested. "There are still quite a few nationalities he hasn't insulted in his lifetime, and this may well be his final chance to cause a scene."

Adding to the concern of palace-watchers the Queen has summoned a priest to be by her husband's side. It is understood she has requested 'no women or Irish' just to be safe.

OUT AT 99: NATION UNSURPRISED AS ENGLISHMAN FAILS TO REACH A CENTURY

People across Australia have today feigned shock at news that an Englishman ended his innings before reaching 100.

"I must admit, it was a bit of a shock," said one pub patron informed of the news. "Normally the Poms are lucky to make it past the 70s. Good on him I say."

Philip will be survived by his Co-Captain Liz whose innings is still going strong, and DNB player Charles.

Philip was expected to attend as guest of honour at The Ashes this year, a visit he is now expected to fulfil in a more personal capacity.

TRIPLE J ANNOUNCE HIP NEW HOST A-DOG JONES

Youth broadcaster Triple J has today revealed their revamped breakfast show lineup, with a new focus on diversity and balance. Head of Triple J, Ita Buttrose, announced she is glad to finally see some fresh faced talent being given a shot in the Australian media industry, with young gun Alan Jones taking over the coveted breakfast slot, after he realised the station has no advertisers to boycott him.

"Yeah guys, I'm just fully stoked to be able to drop some spicy beats and fire bangers for all the Aussie legends out there," said the veteran broadcaster during his first shift on air. "I've been a real fan of the station since it was Single J back in 1923. Anyway enough cheeky bants from me, here's Tame Impala." Although an unorthodox choice for the station, representatives say that Alan will bring a unique set of talents to the role, namely the ability to be handed a fuckload of money from the Liberal Party for absolutely no reason.

"We're really pumped to add A-Dog to our lineup," announced Triple J's new head of programming, Ray Hadley. "His spicy hot takes and strange enthusiasm for the youth market is perfect for a station which has been crucially lacking in the 90-100 demographic."

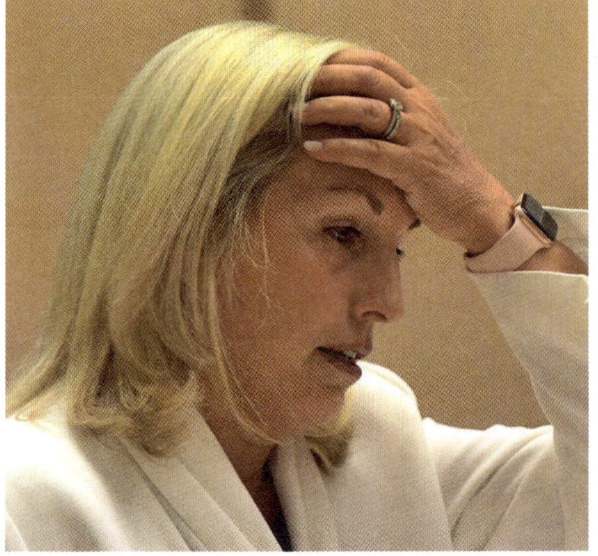

AUSPOST CLAIMS HOLGATE WASN'T HOME WHEN THEY TRIED TO DELIVER HER APOLOGY

The Senate Inquiry into the sacking of Christine Holgate took an unexpected turn late this afternoon, when the chair of Australia Post claimed that he had tried to deliver an apology to the former CEO, but she wasn't home.

However, under intense questioning from cross-bench Senators, it transpired that Lucio Di Bartolomeo did not, in fact, ring on the door bell, nor even walk up the path towards Ms Holgate's house before turning around and taking the apology back to the depot where it remains undelivered to this day.

He did however, fill out a 'Sorry we missed you' card, which he put in her neighbour's letter box. And he later sent her an SMS claiming that the apology had successfully been delivered.

Earlier in the day Ms Holgate testified that, in hindsight, she wished she'd simply sexually assaulted a staff member, which would have resulted in a much lighter punishment.

"LATTES WON'T SOLVE CLIMATE CHANGE" SAYS MAN WHO THINKS MILKSHAKES WILL SOLVE SEXUAL ASSAULT

Prime Minister only man with the power to stop climate change, Scott Morrison, has today blasted inner city voters for being concerned about the insidious threat of ecological collapse that threatens to destroy civilisation as we know it.

"We're not going to achieve net zero in the inner cities cafes," said Morrison. "Those places should be reserved for their traditional purpose of filming weird videos about consent via the medium of milkshakes."

"We're also not going to accomplish a reduction in emissions by charging the biggest polluters and then using the money to subsidise the public who might be charged extra for green energy. That stupidly logical plan has Labor written all over it. Instead what we'll do is replace the good parts in the plan with a copper network so it will only cost three times as much and get rolled out 10 years late. It's a completely foolproof plan."

When asked if they thought drinking lattes and wine in the inner city was going to have an effect on climate change voters were surprised. "No I didn't really think I was stopping climate change by sitting around talking about it in a cafe," said one woman. "I thought I was preventing climate change by advising my friends to only invest my super into ethical power sources, which combined with millions of other inner city voters will force industry change in the absence of any real action from the Federal Government. Because it seems we're not going to achieve net zero in the inner city Canberra buildings either."

'ABC ISN'T EFFICIENT' SAYS GOVERNMENT SPENDING $3.7 MIL ON A MILKSHAKE AD

The government has today slammed the ABC for wasteful spending and inefficiency, stating that the government broadcaster which produces 12 radio stations, 5 national TV stations, a leading national news website, an online streaming service, and a host of social media accounts for $900 million should be more like the 3 minute completely incomprehensible ad they made for a mere $3.7 million.

"Why if the ABC used our efficient spending model they'd be producing almost 36 hours of TV a year!" said one government minister.

The public has meanwhile expressed shock that the government who pre-announced a budget surplus which turned out to be a $700 billion deficit, might not be great at budgeting. "I was shocked, they've always told me they're the better economic managers," said one voter. "But somewhere between Josh Frydenberg misplacing $60 billion, and their 'cheaper' copper NBN which almost doubled the price, I've started to get an inkling that they might not be so great with money after all."

The government has stated that it has learned from this mistake, pledging that in the future it will seek to gain greater efficiencies with its spending, by giving the $3.7 million to News Corp and not asking for anything in particular in return.

DICTATOR DAN STRIKES AGAIN AS PERTH GOES INTO 3 DAY LOCKDOWN

The state of Perth has fallen to the insidious insurgence of Dictator Dan today, after the state declared a complete communist overthrow under the guise of a short 3 day lockdown.

"Ha ha! You all thought I was crippled in a hospital with a serious back injury, but that was just a ruse!" said Dan via the emergency broadcast system today. "Now I will force you all into subservience with my competent governing and people-first health policies, which was my secret devious plan all along!"

Terrified citizens of Perth have flocked to the street in panic, letting off confetti and fireworks in a presumed show of terror. "Oh good, I love Dan," said one clearly brainwashed victim. "I'll do whatever we can do to keep this virus under control."

MORRISON CLARIFIES WHEN HE SAID THE ALMIGHTY MADE HIM PM, HE WAS TALKING ABOUT MURDOCH

Prime Minister and head of buck passing Scott Morrison has today back-pedalled on claims that he was made Prime Minister by a 'higher power' after explaining that he was actually talking about News Corporation. "Oh no, you've got me all wrong," Morrison frantically explained to the press today. "When I said the 'big man from the sky' I was talking about Sky News!"

However, the public has remained sceptical about whether the PM is trying to spin himself out of another crisis, with a few explanations not holding much water. "What about that part where he said when he's been going around forcefully touching people he's actually trying to heal them through prayer?" asked one confused citizen. "I know he tried to backpedal and explain that when he touched that woman he was actually just trying to assault her, but I think he's just saying that because it's clearly more acceptable to the Liberal Party's voters."

35 MAY

Scott Morrison scraps US sub deal in favour of cutting-edge coal powered submarines

'AUSTRALIA NEEDS MORE JESUS' SAYS PM WHO WOULD HAVE JESUS LOCKED UP IF HE CAME HERE

Televangelist Scott Morrison has once again reaffirmed his position that there should be no separation between Pentecostal church and state while doing his campaign tour of churches this week.

During an event speaking at the Christian Conference on the Gold Coast, the PM made the claim that 'Australia needs more Jesus', which he later clarified as meaning 'Australia needs more refugees locked up in detention'.

"How great is Jesus?" asked Morrison, "Sure, he was a poor middle eastern refugee, born to a single mother out of wedlock, raised to be a carpenter, called for everyone to respect the planet, pushed a socialist agenda, believed sex workers deserve respect and was against discrimination. But he has a real impact on how I write policy, minus all that stuff."

"What Australia needs right now is some good old fashioned Christian values," continued the leader who has aided in the cover up of sexual assault allegations against several of his fellow MPs. "Lies, greed, lust, jealousy, none of these have a place in this country, excluding parliament of course."

The PM then went on to hint at a new plan for the nation called 'JesusKeeper' along with it's slogan, "Putting the Christ into Christmas Island".

Man placed under pre-emptive quarantine after visiting five Bunnings in a single day

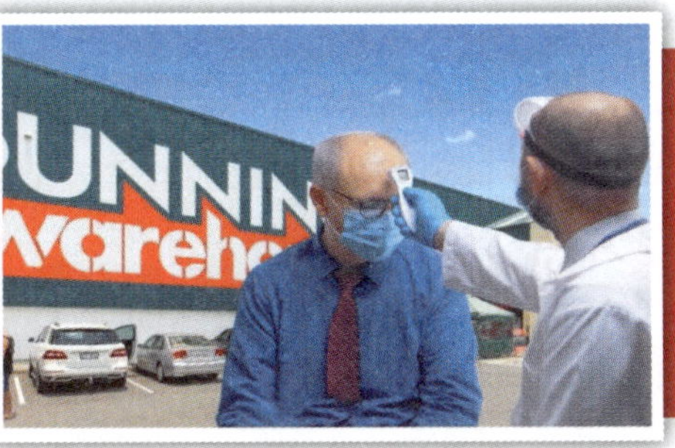

As the outbreak in Sydney's Eastern Suburbs worsens, public rush to panic buy cocaine, botox and gluten-free bagels

Gladys considers stepping down to spend more time with her paper shredder

NATION THAT LOST A WAR TO EMUS RECKONS IT CAN TAKE ON CHINA

The Australian government has today celebrated the first day of their withdrawal from an 8 year losing conflict in Afghanistan by immediately trying to pick a fight with an even more powerful adversary best known for its ability to build entire cities in a week.

"Yes we may have failed to win a war with a ramshackle government in the middle east despite the support of the world's largest military, but I'm sure taking on China would be a walk in the park," declared Peter Dutton today before breaking down in tears over some mean tweets. "Just because we lost the Korean War, Vietnam, Afghanistan, Gallipoli, and that war against a bunch of flightless birds, doesn't mean it won't be eighth time lucky."

However, some Australians have held out some reservations, expressing war with China might not be the smartest geopolitical move. "Fucking what!?!" said one impartial observer. "Yea sure, we can't even build a fucking submarine or a helicopter than can fly at night but lets pick a fight with the world's largest standing army and a cyber army that could cripple our power network in two minutes. I'm sure that'll go really well for a country that can't even roll out cable internet without fucking it up."

"If anybody wants me I'm taking an indefinite holiday in New Zealand."

Government that "can't afford JobKeeper" magically finds $6 billion to give to coal companies

36 **Jeff Bezos tragically survives space flight**

SCOTT MORRISON EMBARKS ON MISSION TO THE SUN AFTER LEARNING IT'S MADE OF NATURAL GAS

Australian gas giant Scott Morrison has journeyed on a solo space mission to the Sun today, after learning it is made of natural gas.

Scott made the amazing discovery today whilst doing a photo-op in a Year 4 science lesson. Upon hearing the news Scott immediately boarded a rocket and piloted it toward the star with a spacesuit helmet in one hand, and a lump of coal in the other.

The mission was cut short however when Morrison was forced to turn back to Earth after Mission Control reminded him that the Sun is also useful for renewable energy such as solar power.

Upon arriving home, Morrison was stopped at the Australian border by Peter Dutton who needed to ensure that Morrison was not bringing any illegal aliens into the country.

When asked why he thought it was possible to fly into the Sun in the first place, Morrison responded that his foolproof plan was to embark on the mission at night while the Sun was dark and cold.

CONFUSED PETER DUTTON ANNOUNCES SPACE FORCE TO KEEP OUT ILLEGAL ALIENS

Minister for Defence Peter Dutton has today emerged from his lair to announce a new wing of the defence force, aimed at keeping out illegal aliens arriving here by ship.

"I have it on good authority that aliens are now trying to sneak past our border by flying in on ships from outer space," said Dutton pointing to conclusive proof he found on a Qanon chatroom. "Rest assured no matter whether you come here by boat, plane, spaceship, you won't be settled here. Unless the alien is working as an au pair, then it's fine."

Asked whether he might be getting his hated asylum seekers mixed up with fictitious Martians from outer space, Dutton asked staff for clarification, before confirming as long as their skin is green then they still won't pass the immigration department's intensive "how white is your skin" test.

ATO to reclassify houses as luxury items **37**

JUNE

Party that covered up a rape for two years demands immediate action against liking tweets

Billionaire who beats up the mentally ill somehow not the villain of movie

Morrison pledges to pray extra hard that someone will help Biloela family

LAZY ENTITLED PARENT TOLD TO GET A JAB

Young people around the country have today urged their parents to put down the avocado toast, stop being so entitled and go out and get a jab. This comes after research suggests nearly 30% of Australians are now hesitant to get the life saving vaccine over a blood-clotting risk potentially high as 0.0017%, which has led older generations to put off getting a jab in favour of sitting at home and getting drunk on vintage red wine.

"Have you bothered to go get a jab yet?" said Mike a 26 year old after getting home today to find their parent on the couch. "All you do is sit around watching TV! It's time you started acting your age and got a vaccine! I don't care if it isn't your dream vaccine, it is at least a vaccine that works. Go now, it's for your own good."

"Classic old people, they are just so entitled these days," said Lauren a 20 year old full time-student, "they just expect everything to be handed to them. They have been spoiled their entire lives and now they refuse to do anything for themselves."

"First the housing market and now vaccines, they just hoard everything for themselves even if they don't actually want to use it. What a selfish and rude generation they are!"

Federal government clarifies whether young people are eligible to get vaccinated

Barnaby Joyce Appointed To Status Of Women Taskforce. Says He Hopes Current Status Is "Single"

Keneally claims she is a diverse candidate: 'I love Vietnamese food'

ABC SUFFERS HUMILIATING BIG FUCKING WIN OVER PORTER

ABC News has been left with their tails between their legs today, after embarrassing themselves by winning a fucking huge victory in the defamation proceedings brought against them by former Attorney General Christian Porter.

The win comes after a settlement deal initiated by Porter and his lawyers the day before evidence against him was due to be revealed in court, in a country where Porter himself has said defamation law is heavily weighted in favour of the plaintiff, which has now left real concern as to the integrity of the ABC and begs the question 'What is it they are trying to hide?'

Reports of the settlement have humiliated the ABC and their editorial standards, if you ignore the fact that Porter settled the case to avoid their 'truth' defence being tested in court.

Reporters from NewsCorp immediately jumped on the opportunity to dunk on the ABC, kicking the ABC while they were on top. "The public broadcaster breaking important stories about the then top law officer in the country and then standing by their reporters until coming out with the win is a complete waste of taxpayer money." explained one News Corp journo. "We'd never do that here."

Government solves mouse plague by releasing a million cats into the wild

Sydneysiders Not Allowed To Leave Metro Area Unless It's To Visit The Gravestone Of An English Relative Who Died 190 Years Ago

AUSTRALIA IN TROUBLE AFTER LEARNING THEY CAN ONLY SEND VACCINATED ATHLETES TO OLYMPICS

The Australian Olympics Committee has decided to send Australia's only vaccinated Olympian, Jan, 71, to Tokyo this year, after a botched vaccine rollout saw every other athlete barred from the event.

"Jan is Australia's oldest, and now only, professional synchronised swimmer," said AOC President Matt Carroll. "It's exciting for us to be able to provide an opportunity like this to an athlete in an often-overlooked age bracket and we look forward to the wisdom and long, rambling tales about old times that Jan can contribute to the team."

While the government has not stated their opposition to vaccinating the rest of Australia's Olympic team, they were unable to confirm that there were 2000 vaccines in the country.

While most of Australia's athletes have expressed dismay at the decision, Jan could not be more excited. "I'm just so happy I can finally take my 5 minute aquatic tribute to Alan Jones international," said Jan. "Plus I heard the parties in the athletes village can be quite the experience, so I've brought a travel bag full of condoms just in case."

PM ANNOUNCES 'BLAMESEEKER' PROGRAM TO FIND WHO SCREWED UP OUR COVID RESPONSE

Prime Minister Scott Morrison has stepped up to address the country's lacklustre response to the covid outbreak, by announcing a program designed to point the blame for Covid away from himself. In a press conference earlier today, the PM announced a new program he has dubbed 'BlameSeeker' which will seek out potential individuals and groups who are likely responsible for Morrison's failures.

"Like all our Covid responses so far, we are excited today to announce a plan and then do nothing to follow through with it," said the PM while browsing holiday deals on his phone, "thanks to BlameSeeker we can finally figure out where our gold standard plan went so wrong. Not pointing fingers, but I'm guessing it had something to do with Dan Andrews."

In response to this unexpected announcement, state leaders have come out and clarified there has been no plan for an actual rollout of BlameSeeker, no new doses of blame to seek out, and no guidelines for the seekers to properly attribute blame safely. Morrison said he has already launched an investigation into this stuff-up, and will he will be coming down hard on anyone he can shift the blame to.

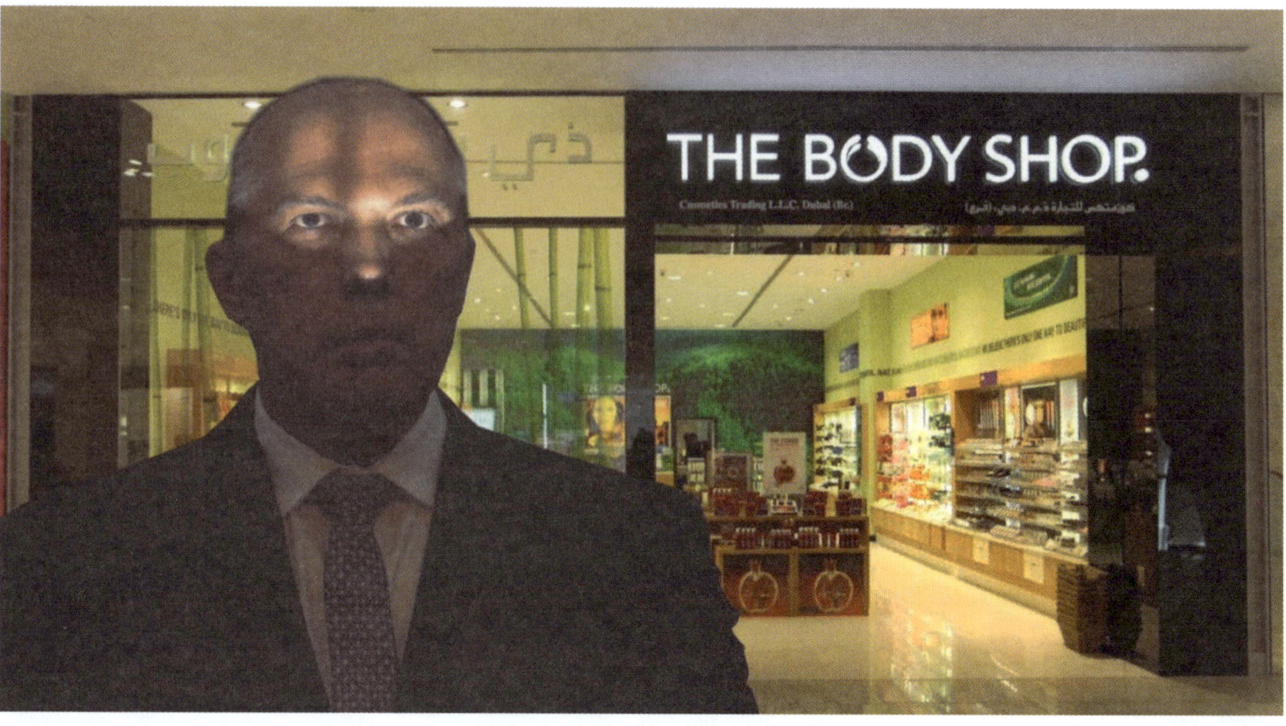

PETER DUTTON SUES THE BODY SHOP FOR FALSE ADVERTISING

Federal Minister and thing that goes bump in the night, Peter Dutton, has today risen from a deep slumber to serve pestilence on mankind, after being informed by servants that the local Body Shop is all out of bodies.

"Vwat do you mean zer is no bodies! Now what am I supposed to ressurrect?" Dutton was heard screaming from the highest tower of his castle. "You shall suffer for this Igor! Bring me my favorite cat of 9 tails immediately."

Dutton was even more upset to learn that his local second hand store was completely out of hands. "I will destroy you and everyone you've ever loved" Dutton was heard to yell at the cashier, "but first how much is this touch lamp?"

CRISTIANO RONALDO BECOMES FIRST FOOTBALL PLAYER TO REFUSE A LINE OF COKE

Soccer player Christiano Ronaldo has today been handed a Guinness world record, after becoming the first ever elite sports person to turn down a line of coke when it was placed in front of him.

However, Ronaldo has since handed back the world record to Guinness, stating he prefers to only take awards from water companies.

The rejection by Ronaldo, which wiped almost $5 billion off Coke's shareprice, has since seen Coke's stock value recruited by Manchester United after the team captain was very impressed by their ability to take over-dramatic dives.

Meanwhile Coca-Cola has sought to reclaim their share price with a new endorsement from the Adelaide Crows. A spokesman for the company said it was a natural fit, as everybody knows those guys never say no to Coke.

Annastacia Palaszczuk to compete in Olympic archery after drawing incredibly long bow over reason she needed vaccine first

JULY

Berejiklian Covid presser goes viral for her amazing impression of Riddler from Batman

ADF put in charge of vaccine rollout to ensure civilians get shot

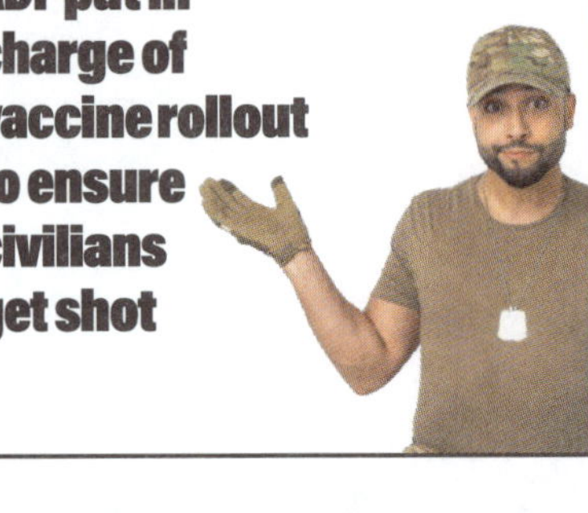

Tourism Aus relaunch 'Where the Bloody Hell Are You' as search for ScoMo continues

DAN ANDREWS OUTWITS SKY NEWS BY LITERALLY GROWING A BACKBONE

Victorian Premier and part time Dictator, Dan "Gulag" Andrews, has today resumed his reign of terror, after successfully taking Sky News's advice to grow a backbone.

The "Melbourne monster", who has spent the last 4 months launching brutal occupations of disabled parking spots, used his first press conference since suffering an evil spinal injury to laugh maniacally for two hours straight, before announcing the entire nation would immediately be plunged into lockdown.

Analysts for Sky News have described the move as "sensible" and "extremely level headed", stating that although they were previously against lockdowns, now that Gladys has been forced to do it, they must therefore actually be a good thing, and everyone should be doing it.

"Golly gosh isn't that Dan a fine upstanding fellow," explained Alan Jones this afternoon. "Why I would vote for him. As should every one of those weirdos on Facebook who can't discern between satire and real news. Boy, it sure would be a shame if I were to influence their votes."

THE CHASER NEWS IN BRIEF

JULY

NSW denies ignoring health experts, stating their decisions were based on the advice of the world's best spin doctors

Acting Prime Minister Barnaby Joyce announces he has cleared his desk to make way for day to day affairs

Budget 2021 Winners and Losers

By Josh Frydenberg

Dear Voter,

As Treasurer of Australia, I was proud to hand down the 2021 Budget on Tuesday night. As you would have read in your local Murdoch press, the most important thing to focus on in any budget is not its broader impact on how it affects society, but its direct impact on you and only you.

With that in mind, here's a list of the pros and cons of our latest budget.

Good news for owners of gas-fuelled power plants! We've propped up your crumbling business for a few extra years. You know what to do when the hat is being passed around at our next fundraising dinner. (Remember the election's really soon!) See you there!

Bad news for people who live on earth and don't want to burn in a fiery hellscape. Unfortunately, we've found people like you don't turn up to our fundraisers, so there's not a lot we could do for you. Perhaps consider getting a second air conditioner for your bedroom?

Good news for people who want to borrow 98% of the cost of your house. Have fun paying that off!

Bad news for investment property owners who get sick of having to list all the tax deductions on their tax returns each year. There will be no relief from all the deductions you get, I'm afraid.

Good news for people who like going overseas. You've got a whole extra year to prepare for your next trip. So get planning now!

Bad news for business executives who hate having to travel to meetings overseas. Unfortunately our exemption system means that you can still come and go as you please. Just make sure you're not wanting to re-enter Australia out of love for your family. In that circumstance, I'm afraid you'll have to go to the back of the queue.

Good news for old people stuck in aged care. At the moment 41% of you are malnourished. With our cash splash that represents roughly a quarter of the funding that's actually needed, the number of people starving should plummet to about 31%. Imagine that — less than a third of you will go to bed hungry each night. What a win!

Bad news for people who visit old people in aged care facilities. You'll still need to remember to take snacks!

Anyway, there's also another $9 billion or so in surprises that we can announce in the lead up to the election using the 21 slush funds we set up that allows ministers to arbitrarily spend your money. So fingers crossed you live in a marginal Liberal electorate. Haha. Not joking though.

Have a great weekend!

Josh Frydenberg
Federal Treasurer

SYDNEYSIDERS TOLD TO STAY HOME UNLESS ATTENDING A SEARCH PARTY FOR SCOTT MORRISON

The New South Wales government has today reiterated to citizens that it is imperative that they stay home and isolate, unless they are the Prime Minister, in which case that particular person should really make an effort to be seen in public more.

"We know that this disease is hiding out there in the community somewhere," explained the NSW Premier today. "So if you see him please tell him to call us because he's supposed to be organising the vaccine rollout."

"We really want to emphasise to the Prime Minister that our limit on being in a room of no more than 10 people doesn't apply to press conferences. Just because 10 journalists turned up doesn't mean you can just go home."

"If anyone has seen him, please be sure to call crime stoppers, his family are worried and colleagues report he hasn't turned up to his job for days."

Friend suggest he may be in the company of a Mr Pfiezer Vaccine, who also went missing earlier in the year. Fearing the worst, police have organised a search party to comb the beaches of Hawaii.

TASMANIAN PREMIER CALLS URGENT PRESS CONFERENCE JUST TO FEEL INCLUDED

Tasmanian Premier Peter Gutwein has today called a 5pm press conference to announce nothing in particular, after feeling fed up that the other states are getting all the attention.

"Typical, after years of everyone making fun of Tasmania for being behind the rest of the country, for once we're leading the pack, and no one gives a shit," he opened in a bizarre tirade. "I haven't got to do one of these all pandemic. Gladys gets to do one every week, and Dan's becoming an insufferable brag. I just want to announce something."

Asked if there was a point to the press conference, or if the press can just go home, Gutwein started pouting. "Fine, you want restrictions? Okay how about this, all three attendees will have to wear masks at the festival of Voices. And you know something else? Footy's cancelled. See, I can be a mean Premier too."

The South Australian Premier also announced a pointless press conference, but no one cared enough to report on it.

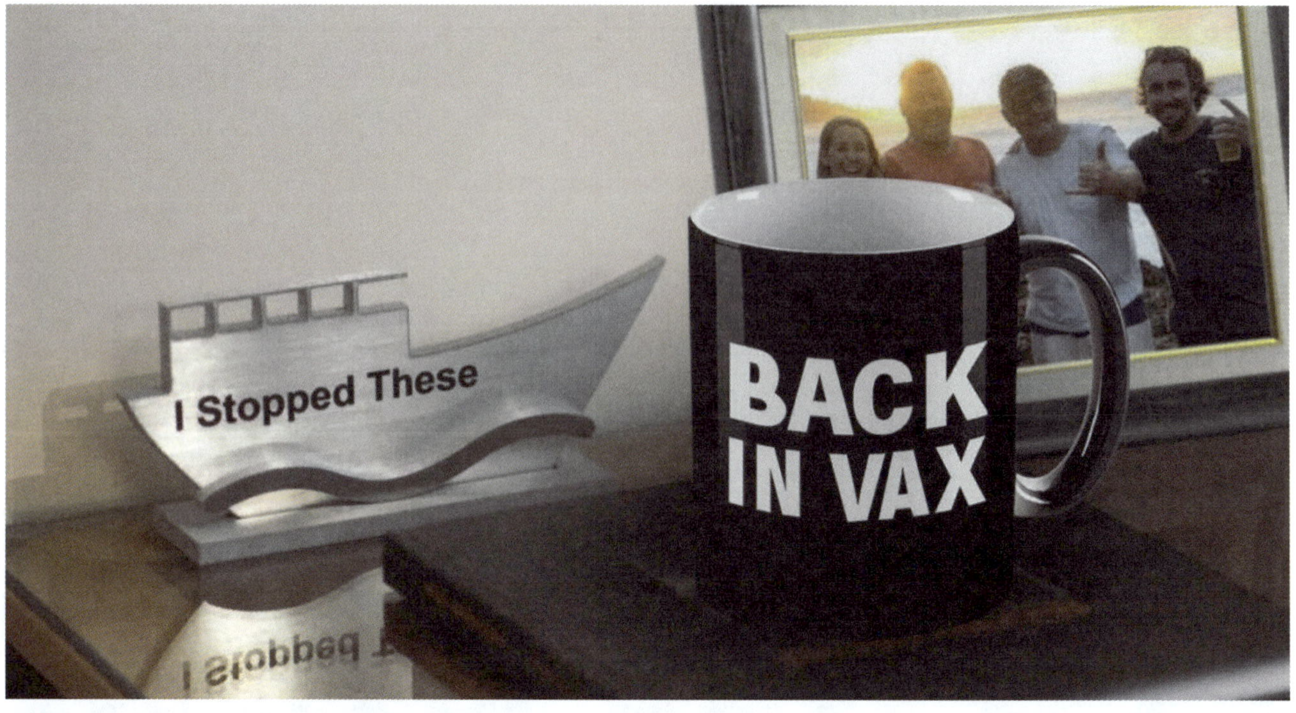

SCOTT MORRISON ANNOUNCES HE'S FULLY VACCINATED THE COUNTRY NEXT YEAR

Prime Minister Scott Morrison has allayed the nation's COVID fears today, by announcing that he has already vaccinated the entire country, next year.

"We've already administered 3 billion shots!" announced Treasurer Josh Frydenberg today. "Whoops, sorry bit of a rounding error there in my maths. Three, we've administered *three* shots."

However some critics have attempted to play down Australia's latest vaccine success story, by pointing out that Australia is the least vaccinated country in the developed world, and the constructs of time make the Prime Minister's announcement physically impossible.

Opposition leader Anthony Albanese has raised concerns that the Prime Minister may have simply been listening to his Qanon mate too much lately, and that there's been a concerning amount of smoke pouring out from under the PM's door.

Mr Morrison has rushed to shut down fears over any delays, pointing out that there is no need to worry and that when he announced the budget surplus a bit early during the last election "everything worked out fine."

BARNABY JOYCE BLAMES OCEAN FIRE ON LACK OF OCEAN BACK-BURNING

Climatologist and social activist Barnaby Joyce has blasted the occurrence of an ocean-fire on the Gulf of Mexico today, stating this whole disaster could have been avoided if only the government had allowed more back burning on the ocean.

"The science is incredibly simple," reasoned Joyce, starting a wild bushfire in his office to illustrate. "If they hadn't left all this highly flammable water lying around we wouldn't have this problem! Back burning is the most effective means for preventing common natural disasters like this, so if anything we should be burning more ocean, not less."

GOVERNMENT INVESTIGATING WHETHER COVID-19 CAN BE BOUGHT OFF WITH $5 MILLION CARPARK

As the Covid-19 pandemic continues to spread across Australia despite over 7% of the population having been vaccinated, the government is now looking into radical new measures to contain the virus, investigating whether it could somehow be convinced to go away if it's given a $5 million swimming pool.

"It's a bit unprecedented, I know," a senior minister told press today. "That sort of money is supposed to go to marginal seats around election time, not towards dealing with highly-infectious respiratory diseases. But it's starting to become clear that the government's present strategy of blaming state Premiers and watching Origin hasn't been as effective as first projected, so we're changing course. Funding expensive sports infrastructure for our mates is all many of our ministers know, it has had great success in saving us from car crash elections in the past, perhaps it'll save us from this slow-motion train wreck too."

BRAD HAZZARD ANNOUNCES PLAN FOR COLOSSEUM IN WHICH UNDER 25S WILL FIGHT FOR PFIZER

Following comments describing the vaccine rollout as "the Hunger Games" NSW Health Minister Brad Hazzard has today announced a new health plan which will see Olympic Park converted into a Colosseum, in order to finally give young people the chance to get vaccinated, by fighting for one of the country's 3 vials of Pfizer vaccine.

"It's a foolproof solution!" explained Hazzard. "We'll solve the problem of there not being enough vaccines for young people, and everyone else gets free entertainment. Plus it'll free up a lot more housing for rich investors that a handful of greedy Millennials selfishly bought up to 'live in'. So there's literally no downside for anyone!"

Update: The three Pfizer vaccines have now been taken off the table, after an elderly Facebook user refused to take anything but the Pfizer vaccine. The three surviving under 25s have been placed back at the end of the queue.

'But I Haven't Done Anything!' Morrison cries as latest poll numbers released

GOVT ANNOUNCES 'LIMBTAKER' SO YOUNG PEOPLE CAN PAY AN ARM AND LEG TOWARDS A HOUSE

The Australian government has announced a new scheme to help young people afford a down payment on a house, declaring 'Limbtaker' will revolutionise home ownership.

The scheme, suggested by Peter Dutton, will allow young people dip into a revenue source they currently don't have access to, their own limbs, by literally buying one arm and one leg from the young person as a down payment on a house.

"It's a great leg up into the market" explained MP Tim Wilson. "Or at least it would be if they hadn't sold that leg."

"As someone who owns 5 houses myself, I understand the struggles young people are facing," he continued. "Why when I told the bank I was looking at a sixth house, the bank went out of the way to make it hard for me, with them saying 'don't you have enough' and 'maybe leave some for others' so I can really relate to young peoples' struggles."

The plan to convince young people to sever off their own limbs in order to help rich people earn a bigger return on investment from the property market, has been hailed as a great success by boomers everywhere, who are set to greatly profit from the move.

"This scheme is about putting your best foot forward to set up your future," said one real estate agent in between doing nothing to fix any rental properties he manages. "I do mean 'best foot quite literally', we want your best foot."

VICTORIAN CONTACT TRACERS RACE TO CONTAIN NEW OUTBREAK OF SCHADENFREUDE

Shops across Victoria have seen their shelves stripped of popcorn today, following the latest COVID outbreak in the "gold standard" state of NSW.

"Wow, escalating cases, that's terrible," said Victoria collectively after having watched the NSW government shrug off multiple outbreaks. "Who would have thought not having a mask mandate, nobody getting vaccines, and everyone being encouraged to just go about their lives would have not been an effective strategy to stop the Delta strain."

"You're all so lucky not to live under the brutal reign of a dictator premier who wants you all to stay healthy and safe. Oh wait now your premier is having to lock down too? Gee I hope you enjoy us sending journalists to all your press conferences then trying to undermine the government's health response. Or is that only okay when you guys do it?"

THE CHASER NEWS IN BRIEF

JULY

Labor organises focus group to find out if it's true they're too reliant on focus groups

Scott Morrison awards self green energy grant after successfully gaslighting the country

Dear Minister Hunt,

Seeing as you're the health minister of your nation, we thought this letter about a life-saving drug we've developed, might be of interest to you.

But we've been trying to contact you for six weeks, and we keep getting palmed off onto junior bureaucrats who have no decision-making power. We're kind of busy (there's a pandemic on), so we really need to talk to people who have the power to make decisions.

Look, I understand you've got a lot going on at the moment too. The distraction of the pandemic is a perfect opportunity to shovel money to the fossil fuel industry, and appoint your gas industry mates to oversee the recovery.

Plus you've got all that Twitter porn to browse. (Sorry, I mean, you have all those 'hackers' to deal with. Ha ha.)

And look, fair enough for using a once-in-a-lifetime health emergency to line the pockets of your business mates. I'm the powerful CEO of a major pharmaceutical corporation. I understand unbridled misuse of power to make up for psychological deficits caused by being teased as a kid. For me it's about price gouging on life-saving medications, leveraging people's desperation to live to juice our bottom line. For you, it's destroying the planet and looking at porn, I get it.

I just kind of think that on this occasion, you are being paid $350k a year to kind of answer our emails. In fact, if there's only one single thing that you do this year, it should probably be answer our fucking email. That single act is basically worth $350k you're being paid.

Look, I'm sure it'll be alright. I mean, what's the worst that can go wrong in 2021? As long as you really work hard on your other responsibility (working out a way to stop the constant leaks from hotel quarantine) I'm sure everything will be fine.

Oh, and good luck with the gas-led recovery. Fingers crossed the next generation doesn't start summarily executing people who wilfully contributed to climate change this late in the piece, eh?

Yours sincerely,

Albert Bourla
CEO of Pfizer Corp

SKY NEWS SLAMS KEVIN RUDD FOR NOT SECURING VACCINES EARLIER

Sky News broadcaster Peta Credlin has today called on Kevin Rudd to resign immediately over the bungled vaccine rollout which saw the former Prime Minister fail to deliver a single vial of vaccine or build a single quarantine facility since the pandemic began.

"The media's silence on Mr Rudd's failure is deafening," Credlin told viewers today. "Maybe if they'd been a bit more like Sky, and spent a little more time focusing on former Prime Ministers instead of the so called 'current government' and their 'responsibility' then we could actually get to the bottom of just how much this is all Labor's fault."

"Why, for example, did Mr Rudd wait until June this year to step in and secure extra Pfizer vaccines to make up for the government forgetting to do so?" continued Credlin. "Why didn't he do this twelve months ago, when he could have saved the government all this embarrassment? Typical selfish Rudd, only thinking about himself and 25 million other Australians. Well I for one have had a gutful."

"Now in other breaking news, benevolent Premier Gladys Berejiklian has continued with another day of sensible and well planned out lockdowns across her state, while Dictator Dan Andrews continues his brutal crusade by closing the Victorian border. More on that after this short 12 minute ad break."

RUDD CONTINUES TO THROW SHADE AT SCOMO WITH INCIDENT-FREE PURCHASE OF BIG MAC VALUE MEAL

Kevin Rudd has today told Scott Morrison to "suck on this sauce bottle" after successfully purchasing a meal at Engadine Maccas without any further incident.

"I'll take one extra spicy McCurry please, and a smoothy to go," said Rudd while staring directly into Scott Morrison's eyes. "Oh, also throw in a napkin for my friend here, he appears to be sweating."

The move is just the latest in an escalating war between former Prime Minister Rudd and Mr Morrison, following a clash which saw the two duke it out over who is best friends with the CEO of Pfizer.

"OMG so like I know I said I was like totes besties with Kev, but I'd never go behind Scott's back like that, like that would be so not cool," said the CEO Albert Bourla today. "Sike, just kidding, LOL as if I would hang out with that loser, I wouldn't even lend him a gel pen, my vaccine gift was totes all because of Kev, he's such a babe, like OMG."

TURNBULL DECIDES TO SORT OUT VACCINES BY JUST BUYING THE WHOLE PFIZER COMPANY

Former Prime Minister Malcolm Turnbull has today one-upped his peers, by just purchasing the entire Pfizer company and calling it a day. "Honestly, I don't know why you guys didn't think of this," said Turnbull. "It's only a few billion dollars. If you'd just cut back on a few avo toasts we could have had this sorted out in March."

However, the plan has already hit a snag, with Health Minister Greg Hunt stating that it had always been the government's plan for Turnbull to buy the company, and that Turnbull doing this made no difference to their ongoing negotiations. "Yes if you just check the secret Pfizer contract which nobody can see, you'd notice it specifically says that on the 5th of March we'll fuck up the vaccine distribution, then on the 11th of June we will announce an increase in supplies right after Rudd steps in to negotiate, and then on the 13th of June Malcolm will buy the company."

"Then on the 15th Tony Abbott's telegrams will finally arrive asking the company to look into curing swine flu," he continued. "It's all very much been planned from the beginning."

NSW GOVERNMENT FURIOUS AFTER REALISING DAN ANDREWS CALLED THEM SLOW LAST MONTH

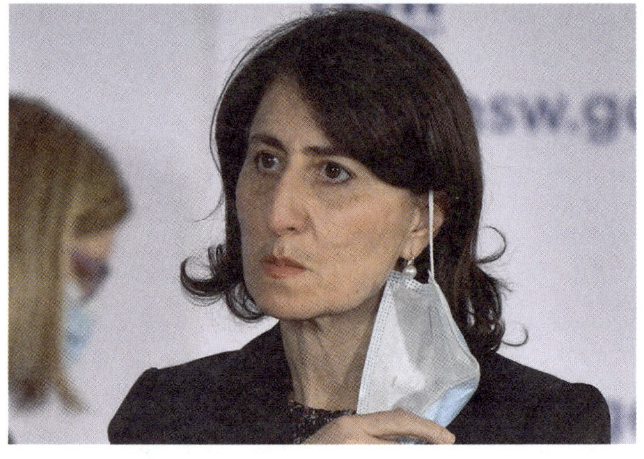

NSW Premier Gladys Berejiklian has today slammed the Daniel Andrews administration, after realising that they accused NSW of being slow to act, during a press conference last month. "I'll have Mr Andrews know that we responded as quickly as humanly possible," explained Mrs Berejiklian in bed later that night, "and I don't think it's very fair to take jabs like that" she continued, while brushing her teeth the next morning.

Upon being told of the retort, Mr Andrews is said to have been surprised. "Huh, what did I say? Oh that thing, but that was three weeks ago?" commented Mr Andrews. "Christ those guys really are slow to respond."

For more breaking updates on this story please check back in 3 weeks for the NSW's governments response

MELBOURNE REBRANDS TO 'HARVEY NORMAN' IN HOPES OF GETTING SOME GOVERNMENT ASSISTANCE

The city of Melbourne has today rebranded as 'Harvey Norman' in hopes it will encourage Morrison government to actually give them some fucking money.

"This is a big day for Melbourne," declared Premier Gerry (formerly Dan), on his way to build carparks in marginal LNP seats to go with their new women's change rooms. "For too long Melburnians have been shafted for government grants simply because we don't own a billion dollar company destroying the planet. Now that we're Harvey Normainians, we are finally flush with cash, just like you'll be flush with cash if you come pick up some great savings on dishwashers this July."

"And while you're here why not consider buying a lovely desks for your more intimate moments?" continued the Premier. "That oughta win over those creeps."

GOVT SUCCESSFULLY SLOWS DOWN DELTA OUTBREAK BY SIGNING IT UP TO THE NBN

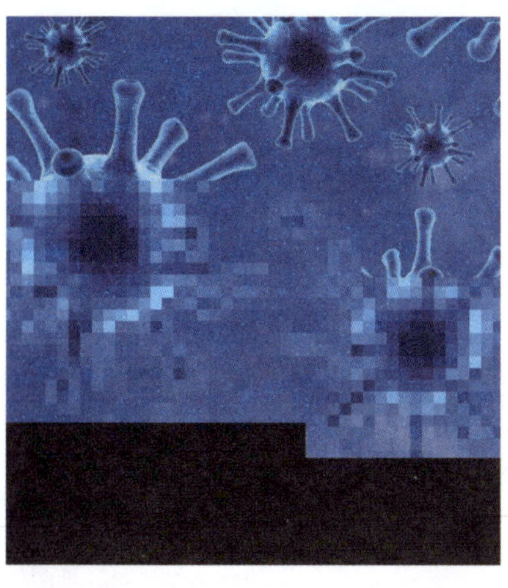

Australians nationwide have sighed a breath of relief today, after the Delta strain of the coronavirus was successfully slowed in its tacks after coming into contact with the NBN.

"It's a miracle," said a woman locked down at home, "finally an actual use for the NBN! I've never been so reli... hello? Sorry I think you dr... no you go. H... hello? Sorry as I was sa..."

However, not everyone is happy with the virus slowdown, with Sky News slamming the Labor party for another failed government rollout. "Typical Labor, promising us 300 cases a day by July then failing to deliver," raged Peta Credlin. "If it weren't for Dan Andrews and his tyrannical lockdowns we're all be enjoying Scott Morrison's quality fibre-to-the-node Covid right now. It's a good thing these vaccines are giving us all free 5G."

An attempt was made to contact Covid for this piece, but no response was received by the time of publication, due to its internet being down following a light breeze

Barnaby retrains as judge after learning they do lots of banging on desks

Sydneysider relieved to have avoided that unnecessary short lockdown in June

"I will not be locked down" says woman who agreed to go on show where you get locked down

FOLLOWING TOKYO'S LEAD, PARLIAMENT TO INSTALL CARDBOARD DESKS TO DISCOURAGE MPS FROM HAVING SEX ON THEM

Exasperated cleaners at Parliament house have today announced that they will be replacing all desks in the building with disposable cardboard replacements until further notice, in order to discourage MPs from doing unspeakable things on them during work hours.

"We will be starting with Barnaby's office, then the prayer room, then pretty much everywhere Christian Porter has allegedly been," said the cleaner. "We'll also be removing all the doors until we know these MPs can be trusted."

The plan follows recent developments at the Tokyo Olympics, which has seen all athletes provided with cardboard, single-sized beds in an attempt to discourage fraternizing. "We simply can't risk the possibility that the athletes could come into contact with each other and cause an outbreak," explained organizers. "While the beds weren't particularly effective in the end, we found installing a picture of Barnaby on the wall has had an 100% success rate at keeping everything in the sleeping quarters purely platonic. It's probably the first time Barnaby's been the solution instead of the cause of a sexually transmitted disease."

THE CHASER NEWS IN BRIEF

AUGUST

Brisbane forced to turn down 2032 Olympics over fears country won't be vaccinated by then

As the UK's Health Minister gets stood down for cheating on his wife, Australian politicians express confusion over why they didn't just promote him to Deputy PM

DAN ANDREWS ANNOUNCES PLAN TO BUILD WALL AROUND VICTORIA AND MAKE SYDNEY PAY FOR IT

Ruthless madman Dictator Dan has once again ramped up his conflict with the democratic and peaceful NSW government, after declaring plans to build a wall around the Victorian border with NSW, a wall he claims will be paid for by Sydney.

"When NSW send us their people they aren't sending their best," he claimed at a rally today. "They're sending Peta Credlin, they're sending Alan Jones. And some, I guess, are good people. But we can't take that chance."

However, concerns are growing among eagle eyed watchers that this may simply be a diversionary tactic to lower NSW's guard before an eventual invasion is launched by the Latte Army.

"We will starve them out by setting up a ring of steel around the city," Dan told his war room today. "We will force a surrender by capturing their most valuable resource – the elite private school kids. At all costs we must try and avoid taking the roads, they are a death trap. The traffic alone is a nightmare and the layout make no sense. Have you seen a map of Sydney, it looks like a toddler drew it. God knows how Covid ever managed to get out."

"WE JUST WANT CLOSURE": PARENTS OF MISSING PRIME MINISTER BEG WITNESSES TO COME FORWARD

Parents of missing boy Scott Morrison have today appealed to the public, asking that anyone who has seen their son in the last month to please contact him and ask him to do his fucking job.

"We're never going to give up hope that our Scott is still out there somewhere," said the victim's parents at a press conference today. "If you're listening Scott, we still love you, we just wish you'd take a few less holidays and maybe call in and let the country know you're still alive at least once a week."

Police are describing the circumstances around the Prime Minister's disappearance as "extremely suspicious" given the timing. "We don't think the fact that he disappeared right as the Olympics is coming up is a coincidence," explained officers, "and we have sent out a team to trawl the baths of Tokyo to see if we can't turn up any evidence. A Bunnings serviette, a floral wraith, a discarded bottle of British Ale, anything that might give a clue as to where he's fucked off to this time."

"Can't you see we're living in a dictatorship" says protester who wants to overthrow democratically elected government and replace it with one of their choosing

SKY NEWS MOVES TO PORNHUB AFTER LEARNING THEY DON'T CENSOR VIDEOS OF MASSIVE DICKS

Since receiving a 1 week suspension from YouTube, Sky News have been forced to find other methods for spreading their important misinformation about Covid-19 to the world. After an entire quarter-hour of brainstorming, Andrew Bolt had decided it was time he launched back in to posting content on his trusty OnlyFans account.

OnlyFans, a platform not shy from promoting footage of gigantic dicks fucking everything, gratefully accepted the diversification of talent, eager to increase their reach in the demographic of people who are willing to pay premium prices for nothing.

The Sky News OnlyFans account now boasts several million followers after they posted their first video of Craig Kelly [redacted]ing a [redacted].

BARNABY PUT ON CASHLESS DEBIT CARD AFTER TURNING UP TO WORK DRUNK

Deputy Prime Minister Barnaby Joyce has been put on a cashless debit card, after he was found to be intoxicated at work yesterday.

The immigrant who has spent a large part of his life living off government money, will now only be able to access funds through the card until such time that he can be trusted to not make decisions, like attempting to murder a Hollywood actor's dogs. His employer, the Australian people, justified the decision in a statement today, explaining that Joyce has a young family relying on him and that he has previously expressed difficulties in making ends meet.

Joyce will be the first person in the Federal Parliament to use the card. However, many of the card's supporters say that it should be extended to the entire building. "This isn't about punishing these people, it's about helping them," explained one concerned citizen. "Booze, sexual assault, drugs – every day it's another shameful story coming out of this place. Not even sacred land like the prayer room is left untouched. Clearly these people can't be trusted to handle their own money, so from now on Centrelink will be overseeing their spending."

Update: Every MP is now in 10,000 debt due to a Robodebt rounding error.

54 **Government announces children as young as 12 will be eligible for a vaccine announcement later this year**

NEW LAND SPEED RECORD REACHED BY PRIME MINISTER RUNNING AWAY FROM RESPONSIBILITY

A new land speed record has been achieved by Scott Morrison this week after Prime Minister Scott Morrison was caught running away from dealing with a disaster. Morrison was clocked breaking the sound-barrier this week when he was asked to give an apology to Australians on the vaccine rollout, to which Scott responded by bolting in the opposite direction.

Running coaches have theorised that Morrison can actually improve on his top speed, and might be able to run faster if his motivation is stimulated further. Experts believe that if Scott is running away from responsibility, and toward a curry lunch photo-op with Brian Houston at a coal-mine where he's announcing a new car park, he could potentially reach the speed of light.

Morrison will now officially be competing in the 2032 Brisbane Olympics, with the proviso he is not held responsible for making sure the games run smoothly.

"GOD WILL SAVE ME FROM THE VIRUS" SAYS CHRISTIAN REFUSING THE VACCINE GOD SENT

Local Christian Mary Thrupple has today turned down a life-saving vaccine, stating that her faith in God is all the protection she needs, much to the surprise of the hundreds of thousands of Christians who have died of Covid so far.

However, representatives for God say that this is a really stupid thing to do, given all the time God put into creating those vaccine scientists to help save Mary from the virus.

"What the heck, I'm literally giving her a miracle cure!?" said an exasperated God watching on from a nearby cloud. "What more does she want me to do, wrap a bow around it and have some cherubs deliver it on a beam of light? Vishnu give me strength, this woman is driving me up the wall."

Asked whether it might just be easier to smite earth and start again from scratch, God said he was seriously considering it. "It was bad enough when they started denying the dinosaurs," he sighed. "After I spent millions of years building those things. I mean, I can understand not believing in an invisible sky man, but not believing in stuff where there's fossil evidence, that's just straight up moronic."

"TEMPORARY" SCHOOL CLASSROOM CELEBRATES TWENTY YEARS SINCE CONSTRUCTION

Staff and students of Average Public High School are in high spirits as they celebrate the 20th anniversary of their temporary demountable classrooms being installed, and 19 years since the school started promising they would be torn down soon.

"Though the classrooms may be temporary, the memories of them will last forever," said the School Principal wistfully. "Why it was in Demountable c3 where I had my very first class – as a student!"

As the school celebrated the milestone anniversary, students took turns sharing their favourite moments that transpired within the gum-plastered walls. Some fan favourites included the Bunsen Fire of '06, the Fan-Collapse of '09, and the time that the teacher rolled in the TV on wheels to play Shrek which is also the only thing any of the students remember from grade 3 math.

When asked if anyone at Average Public knew the definition of the word 'temporary', students pointed out that word is for some reason included in the Google search block list by the state Government. When contacted for comment a Department of Education employee explained the block was only temporary, and therefore would be lifted sometime in the next 150 years.

CENSUS FAILS AGAIN DUE TO HALF OF SYDNEY BEING OUT ON CENSUS NIGHT

The Australia Bureau of Statistics has once again been thrown into chaos tonight, following another census fail that has seen nobody in Bondi fill out the form due to being out on the town.

"These results are a mess!" exclaimed one ABS employee. "Look here, it says 20 million Australians have filled out the form, but our last census in 2016 reported there were only 6 people living here. Something here doesn't add up."

However, some data has been able to be salvaged from the survey, with the ABS successfully learning that 0% of Australians are excited for the Hey Hey It's Saturday reboot, 50,000 couples have recently broken up over the stress of defining their relationship on the census form, and 69% of Australians are immature enough to find childish number gags funny.

The ABS also discovered 100% of people reading this are now consciously aware that they are breathing, and are extremely frustrated for it being pointed out.

PARALYMPICS INTRODUCE NEW 'NDIS' SPORT WHERE CONTESTANTS MUST JUMP THROUGH ENDLESS HOOPS TO QUALIFY

As the Paralympics get underway in Tokyo, Aussie athletes have declared they are more than prepared for the challenge ahead, thanks to years of practice jumping through hoops, being run round in circles, and bending over backwards to qualify for the NDIS.

"We are ready to win," said one athlete after a gruelling session on the phone to an NDIS correspondent, "if I can make it through that interrogation I can get through anything. Besides getting through to actually getting funding obviously."

Australians have already won big in the early competitions, with one gold medal recipient stating that his experience having to jump huge hurdles to qualify for the NDIS helped him stay ready fit for the steeplechase event.

Update: tragedy has struck for the Australian Olympic team after the entire squad was forced to bow out as a result of being deemed to not have a disability by the NDIS

CHANNEL 7 RENAMES 'HOME AND AWAY' TO JUST 'HOME'

Channel 7 has announced its soap opera 'Home and Away' is being renamed to 'Home' due to Covid restrictions. The change is designed to better reflect the world during Covid times, to help the show better relate to the tens of people who still watch free-to-air television.

"We all need to make changes in these times," said a Channel 7 executive, "the show is no different. We have worked hard to make the show as Covid-safe as possible without compromising on the product placement our fans love."

The classic of Aussie television which remains a hit to this day in a large part thanks to 'hit show' being a term that is relative to the amount of people who watch TV, is known for being the only show where if you ask fans why the show is still on air, they talk about actors who were on the show decades ago.

"We have been silenced" says news organisation that owns 81 papers, 21 magazines, 45 TV stations and a cable monopoly after their YouTube is suspended for a week.

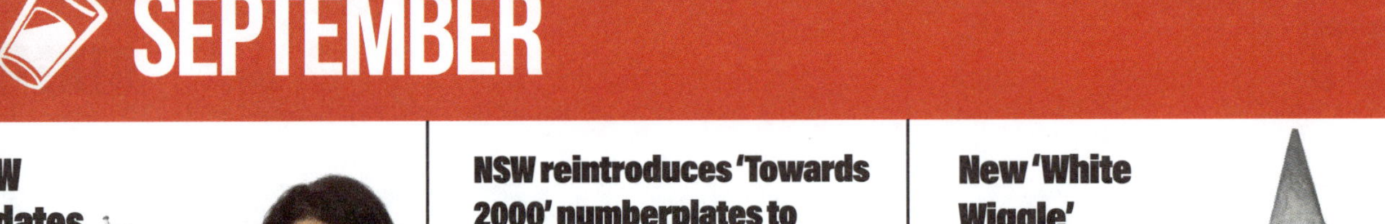

SEPTEMBER

NSW updates state flag

NSW reintroduces 'Towards 2000' numberplates to commemorate upcoming milestone

New 'White Wiggle' introduced to help Matt Canavan feel represented

COVID DECLARES WE MUST LEARN TO LIVE WITH NSW GOVERNMENT

NSW resident, the novel coronavirus, has today held a press conference to inform the public that the situation is now too far gone, and that the people of NSW are just going to have to live with the disease they call a government for at least the next year.

"The fact is nobody could have predicted it would have been this bad," said the defeated virus today. "The best we can hope for now is that everyone be injected with enough knowledge that they'll be able to eradicate this growing problem at the next election. Until then we all just need to bunker down in our homes and ride out the worst of this."

However experts have suggested there were early warning signs of how deadly the NSW government and its Federal variant had become, within days of the latest outbreak. "I think the fact that when the outbreak was occuring, the NSW Nationals were some of the first infected due to holding a gathering in Paddington, and the fact that the Prime Minister was too busy swanning around British pubs to address the situation, and that the Deputy Prime Minister was too busy fighting a leadership spill to deal with the outbreak – these might have been a good indicator of the danger to come," explained one political scientist. "Also simply the fact that they're NSW politicians. That was a bit of a red flag too I guess."

Experts hoping Ivermectin will cure some of Joe Rogan's more horse-shit ideas

Shane Warne tests positive for Covid, herpes, gonorrhea, chlamydia, cocaine...

59 SEPTEMBER

CONSERVATIVE LONGS FOR THE DAYS WHEN WIGGLES UPHELD TRADITIONAL VALUES OF 4 GROWN MEN LIVING TOGETHER IN A HOUSE WITH NO WOMEN

Nationals Senator and coal-miner cosplayer Matt Canavan has today taken some time away from the spiralling health crisis enveloping the nation, to focus on the much more important issue of the diversity of a children's entertainment group.

"It is simply outrageous that the Wiggles would pander to the 80% of their fanbase that aren't white men," said a furious Canavan. "When I sit down to watch my daily Wiggles I expect them to continue to display the conservative values I expect – four grown men in tight rainbow clothing who live together and bond over their love of dance while another man wearing leather pants occasionally comes round to tickle them. You know, traditional values."

Informed that the Wiggles have actually had female members for 9 years now, and that the Wiggles has never had an all-white lineup, Canavan was furious. "Are you telling me that all this time Jeff wasn't white!? I thought he was just doing a hilarious blackface routine!?! What's next, is Sesame Street going to introduce a black couple? That does it, I'm never watching shows designed for 2-year-olds ever again. Your loss Wiggles."

GOVERNMENT BEST KNOWN FOR LOCKING DOWN HALF OF SYDNEY EVERY NIGHT FOR 10 YEARS ANNOUNCE THEY DON'T DO CURFEWS

Premier State and record holder for the world's largest retirement village, New South Wales, has this week demonstrated they have learned absolutely nothing from 10 years of lockdown rehearsals after the state once again racked up record Covid numbers as a result of people visiting others' homes.

"These aren't the numbers we are wanting to see, so can I just say, please know, and that is very concerning," said the Premier today for the 48th day in a row. "And if me standing here and repeating the same sentence every day for two months won't fix the problem I am simply out of ideas. You're all on your own."

Sydney locals meanwhile have flocked to the streets, stating that the instructions 'stay home' were simply too complicated to understand. "Wait so if they said stay home that means I can go to someone else's home right?" asked one Sydneysider who somehow still isn't getting this after two months. "And can I go to Homewares Emporium? That has the word home in it?"

"The fact is I never really wanted to go out before, after all I moved to Sydney for a reason," explained another local on the way to JBHifi. "But now that I've been told I can't go out, I'll be damned if I'm going to let some government 'health expert' tell me I'm not allowed to kill a few elderly relatives."

TASMANIA QUIETLY ENACTS PLAN TO TOW STATE OVER TO NEW ZEALAND

In a decision that was widely protested by competitors of the Sydney to Hobart and nobody else, the state of Tasmania has today left the Commonwealth of Australia. Seeing that the rest of the country was wrapped up in their internal Covid spats, the Island State reportedly seized the opportunity to make a break for New Zealand while nobody was looking, by attaching an outboard motor to the west coast and punting its way across the ditch.

Responding to complaints about the decision, the country's smallest state revealed that it actually announced its plans to leave months ago, but nobody from the mainland had bothered to pay attention to what they were saying.

The decision to migrate the state to New Zealand reportedly came about due to their shared love of being forgotten on maps, their enthusiasm for sheep breeding, and their shared status as places that even COVID-19 would rather not visit.

Residents of Tasmania have stated that by becoming New Zealand citizens, they are looking forward to Australia laying claim to them for the first time in history.

ABBA ANNOUNCE COMEBACK ALBUM 'GRANDMAMMA MIA'

ABBA fans around the globe have rejoiced today, after the group announced it has reformed after 40 years, and will be releasing a new album. Initial reviews for the tracks have been overall positive with fans young and old loving the updated ABBA style. Sources tell us they already are working on a comeback album that is a greatest hits album but re-written to fit the band's current perspective called 'GrandMamma Mia'.

The album will feature a track list including:

Mobility Scooter Queen

Knowing Me, Who Are You?

The Winner Takes All the Hard Candies

Emergency Visit To The Waterloo

Take A Chance on my Grandson, He Is A Nice Boy

Rent Money, Rent Money, Rent Money

Asked what they think about ABBA's unexpected comeback, the bands original fanbase have said 'What? Speak up?'

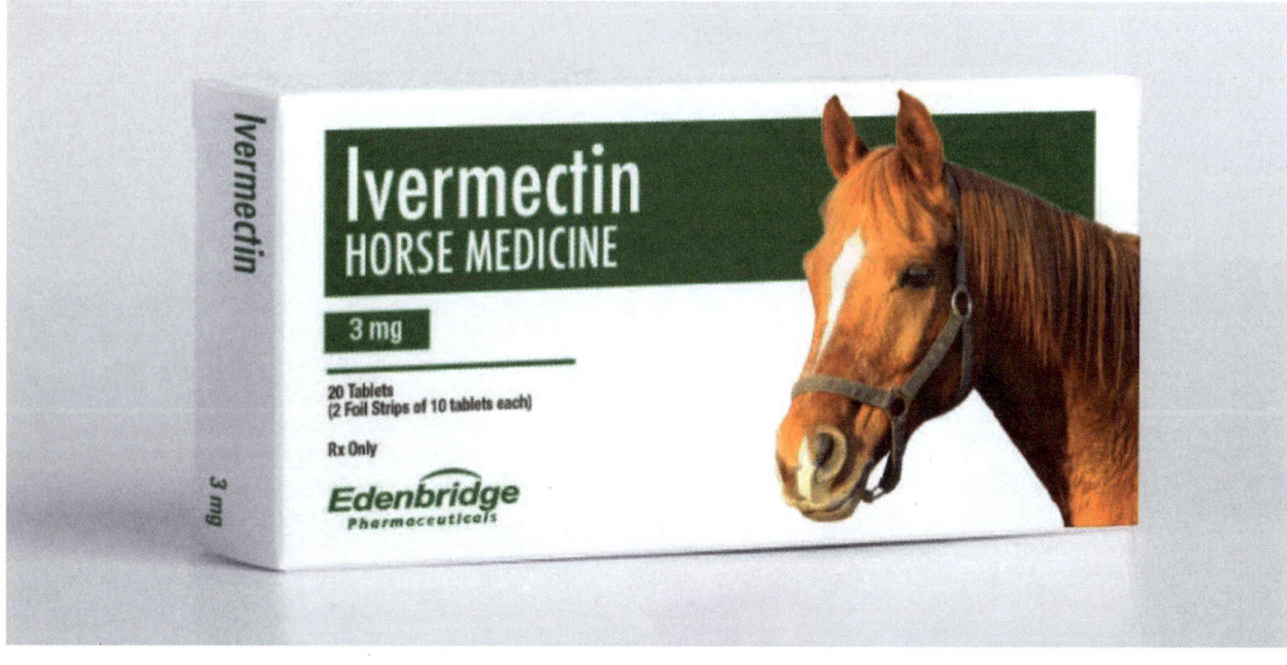

'THIS IS BRILLIANT': CEO OF IVERMECTIN DELIGHTED IDIOTS KEEP EATING HIS MEDICINE

The head of horse deworming brand Ivermectin has encouraged the world's halfwits to keep eating the paste. While making no claims for the product's efficacy in fighting human illnesses, the CEO confirmed that he was able to pay his staff a sizeable bonus this quarter.

In a statement, CEO Graham Martin-Donald said:

"We at Ivermectin would like to thank the fuckwit community for their support."

"Four years ago we were just another brand in the horse-care aisle. Today we can say we are recommended by conservative talk show hosts, Midwestern mayors, disgraced reality TV stars and Australian celebrity chefs-turned cult leaders. Go on, try and name another horse deworming brand. You can't, can you?"

"On a personal note, I don't care why you pea-brains are buying it – just keep buying it. Put it in your food, brush your teeth with it, stick it in a pipe, stick it up your pipe. I don't give a shit. I've just bought another Porsche."

TECTONIC PLATE OFFERED GOVT JOB AFTER BEING A BIT SHIFTY

The Federal cabinet have unveiled their newest recruit today, announcing that the tectonic plates responsible for Melbourne's earthquake would be promoted to Attorney General. The new recruit was reportedly talent scouted by the LNP, after some allegedly 'shifty' behaviour piqued the Liberal Party's interest.

"We're excited to see what skills these plates bring to the table." announced Scott Morrison. "After seeing how unstable and destructive they are, I think they'll fit in well around here."

Not every member of the LNP have thrown their support behind the appointment however, with reports suggesting the tectonic plates have caused fissures within the LNP. Members of the party's right have expressed concerns the newly promoted plates run the risk of destroying the earth and making the planet unliveable, which they explain is actually Matt Canavan's job.

SCIENTISTS' CAREER IN MEDICINE NO MATCH FOR 3 HOURS OF GOOGLE, DECLARES IDIOT

A local idiot has taken to the internet to research the health impacts of COVID and vaccines, and has since come to the sensible conclusion that they are more knowledgeable than doctors and epidemiologists who've spent their life studying these topics, again reinforcing that there's nothing more dangerous than a dipshit with a search engine.

"I've seen a thing or two in my day, and this whole pandemic thing is a load of rubbish," asserted the self-proclaimed 'School Of Life' graduate. "And I'm not the only one who thinks so, you'll find other likeminded geniuses on George Christensen and Pete Evans' Facebook pages who aren't buying into this whole scam-demic."

Following their discovery that the pandemic is a lie and that vaccines cause autism, the internet health-expert took to Google to make more professional diagnoses on the state of their own health. After inputting their symptoms to WebMD, they have now self-diagnosed themselves with Munchausen Syndrome.

LOCAL MAN MORE WILLING TO JOIN UNHINGED CONSPIRACY CULT THAN ADMIT HE'S A BIT AFRAID OF NEEDLES

The Oak Milk corporation has today filed for insolvency, after a Melbourne-wide strike by unvaxinated tradies made the company's future untenable.

"The fact is we've been on the brink for a while now," explained Oak's CEO. "Between the lack of teenagers hanging out at skateparks, no school lunch orders, cricket games being called off, and now tradies also being banned from smokos, well there's almost no customer base left at this point."

"The only product that hasn't been affected are banana milk sales, which have remained consistent at zero for the last ten years."

Meanwhile, tradie favourite the Four'N Twenty pies company has not been nearly affected by the downturn, due to their side business of rodent removal thriving due to the mouse plague. "Yea it's been really good for business," explained Four'N Twenty's head of extermination. "We've saved a thousands of dollars having to source meat."

The Winfields Cigarettes company have reportedly also been placed on life support today, though that's largely just due to the staff consuming too much their own product.

62 **Morrison takes full responsibility for vaccine bungle and offers to take some time off in Hawaii to think about what he's done**

"NO VACCINES FOR MY PURE BODY" DECLARES MAN ON HIS 3RD BIG MAC FOR THE WEEK

NSW to receive $700m disaster relief after Victoria hit by earthquake

MAN WHO BROUGHT IN ROBODEBT COMPLAINS ABOUT BEING PUNISHED FOR BEING GIVEN MONEY HE DIDN'T ASK FOR

Minister for Science Christian Porter has today resigned from cabinet, after the former Attorney General was blindsided by this strange new thing called "rules". Stating that he had no way of knowing that accepting millions in anonymous donations would affect his ability to act as an MP, the minister celebrated his resignation as another humiliating defeat for the ABC's lawyers.

Releasing a public statement this afternoon, Porter lambasted the media for reporting that the country's top legal representative was alleged to have committed a horrible crime. "I can't believe we now live in a world where people are no longer assumed innocent until proven guilty," said the man who oversaw a giant robotic system that hounded poor people to pay debts they never owed. "What kind of monster wouldn't wait for a court ruling before assuming someone had broken the law?"

Asked what he will be doing now that he has stood down, Porter said he is looking forward to spending the next three years on the phone to Centrelink, trying to get them to process his unemployment.

ICUs overrun after launch of Sky News free-to-air leaves thousands braindead

Annual Magazine regrets opting to print book in September

"Black 007 not historically accurate!" says man who worships a white Jesus

NSW replace Premier with looped recording of 'Please Know'

WORLD BRACES FOR 2020: 2

The world has battened down the hatches and stocked up on as much toilet paper as they could find, following reports that they are about to enter 2020:2.

"What, I thought we only just escaped that nightmare!?" screamed one man who has only just worked up the courage to leave the house. "I don't know if I can take that year again. I mean the virus I can deal with, but if the celebrities start singing Imagine again I'm yeeting myself off the face of the earth."

However scientists have rushed to reassure the public that years don't work that way, and they had in fact just misheard the year '2022'. "Let us reassure you that 2022 is a completely different year," said a representative from Greenwich Institute of Timekeeping. "All the tragedies that are about to befall you this year will be much worse than that trial run we called 2020."

"I mean... Happy New Year!"

THE CHASER NEWS IN BRIEF

DECEMBER
Relative who clearly has no idea what your interests are hedges bets with gift of 'The Chaser Annual' for Christmas

YOU'RE ABOUT TO LEAVE THE SHOVEL HALF

WARNING: The Chaser half of this magazine was produced in a "gold standard" state, and therefore is likely riddled with coronavirus.

WARNING: The Shovel side of this magazine is full of references to the most corrupt Premier in a generation. No not the one that got stood down for corruption. The guy that made everyone stay home.

YOU'RE ABOUT TO LEAVE THE CHASER HALF

Tonight, I'll be eating

at the brand new Wagga Clay Target Association Clubhouse

Uber Eats

All the worst parts of capitalism, brought straight to your door